AMERICAN CIVIL LIBE

ACLU

HANDBOOKS FOR YOUNG AMERICANS

The Rights of American Indians and Their Tribes

STEPHEN L. PEVAR

PUFFIN BOOKS

To Lianna, Elena, Benjamin, James,
Daniel, William, Sarah, and Rebecca

PUFFIN BOOKS
Published by the Penguin Group
Penguin Putnam Inc., 375 Hudson Street, New York, New York 10014, U.S.A.
Penguin Books Ltd, 27 Wrights Lane, London W8 5TZ, England
Penguin Books Australia Ltd, Ringwood, Victoria, Australia
Penguin Books Canada Ltd, 10 Alcorn Avenue, Toronto, Ontario, Canada M4V 3B2
Penguin Books (N.Z.) Ltd, 182–190 Wairau Road, Auckland 10, New Zealand

Penguin Books Ltd, Registered Offices: Harmondsworth, Middlesex, England

First published in the United States of America by Puffin Books,
a member of Penguin Putnam Inc., 1997

1 3 5 7 9 10 8 6 4 2

LIBRARY OF CONGRESS CATALOGING-IN-PUBLICATION DATA
Pevar, Stephen L.
The rights of American Indians and their tribes / Stephen L. Pevar ;
foreword by Norman Dorsen.
p.   cm.—(ACLU handbooks for young Americans)
Includes bibliographical references and index.
Summary: A history of federal Indian policy precedes discussion of topics
related to the legal rights of American Indians, including treaties;
tribal self-government; hunting, fishing, and gathering rights; civil rights;
and criminal jurisdiction in Indian country.
ISBN 0-14-037783-2 (pbk.)
1. Indians of North America—Legal status, laws, etc.—Juvenile literature.
[1. Indians of North America—Legal status, laws, etc.]   I. Title.   II. Series.
KF8205.P48   1997   342.73'0872—dc21   97-20124   CIP   AC

Printed in U.S.A.
Set in ITC Century Book

CONTENTS

FOREWORD

This guide sets forth the rights of American Indians and their tribes under the present law and offers suggestions on how they can be protected. It is one of a series of handbooks for young adults which is published in cooperation with the American Civil Liberties Union (ACLU).

This guide offers no assurances that the rights it discusses will be respected. The laws may change, and in some of the topics covered in these pages they change quite rapidly. An effort has been made to note those parts of the law where movement is taking place, but it is not always possible to predict accurately when the law *will* change.

Even if the laws remain the same, their interpretations by courts and administrative officials often vary. In a federal system such as ours, there is a built-in problem since state and federal law differ, not to mention the confusion between states. In addition, there are wide variations in how particular courts and administrative officials will interpret the same law at any given moment.

If you encounter what you consider to be a specific abuse of your rights, you should seek legal assistance. There are a number of agencies that may help you, among them ACLU affiliate offices, but bear in mind that the ACLU is a limited-purpose organization. In many communities, there are federally funded legal service offices which provide assistance to persons who cannot afford the costs of legal representation. In general, the rights that the ACLU defends are freedom of inquiry and expression, due process of law, equal protection of the laws, and privacy. The authors in this series discuss other rights (even though they sometimes fall outside the ACLU's usual concern) in order to provide as much guidance as possible.

These publications carry the hope that Americans, informed of their rights, will be encouraged to exercise them. Through their exercise, rights are given life. If they are rarely used, they may be forgotten and violations may become routine.

It is of special importance that young people learn what their rights are and that there is such a thing as "rights"—individual liberties that the government, no matter how strong, must honor. Only a self-confident country can remain faithful to such a vision, and young people are the future of all countries, whether or not these recognize the value of rights to a thriving civilization. The handbooks in this series are designed to contribute to this goal.

Norman Dorsen
Stokes Professor,
New York University School of Law
President, ACLU 1976–1991

ACKNOWLEDGMENTS

I would like to thank the people whose encouragement and support were so instrumental to the completion of this book. They include my immediate family—Laurel, Lianna, Elena, Micki, Nathan, Peter, Cindy, Dana, and Jeffrey—and my friends—Barbara Barton, Larry Nault, Mike Butyn, King Golden, Stephen Metcalf, Lynn Charles, Mark Perkell, Michael Livingston, Arlynna Howell Livingston, Julian and Diane Spirer, Marshall and Deborah Matz, Joseph McSoud, Mark and Nancy Connell, Hap Patz, Steve Robinson, Brian LeMaire, Dale Britt, David Miller, Barbara Shaw, and Matthew Cohen.

INTRODUCTION

The subject of Indian rights is complex and terribly confusing. There are thousands of treaties, statutes, executive orders, court decisions, and agency rulings that play integral roles. It is one of the most difficult areas of the law to explain, which is one reason why Indians and tribes often have difficulty protecting their rights.

The subject of Indian rights is also highly controversial. Everyone familiar with it seems to have a strong opinion about it. Some people resent the fact that Indians have special hunting, fishing, and water rights, for example. Others feel that Indians are simply exercising rights that have always been theirs.

This book is not written with the idea that Indians deserve better treatment than other people do. It is dedicated instead to a principle: every right you and I have was acquired at a significant cost, paid for either by us or by others to whom that right was worth fighting for. Yet unless we know what our rights are, we cannot exercise them, and unless we exercise them, we may lose them.

AUTHOR'S NOTE

Considerable thought was given to choosing between the terms "Native American" and "Indian" in this book. "Indian" was chosen for several reasons. First, most Indians use "Indian" and "Native American" interchangeably, and most Indian organizations, including the National Congress of American Indians and the American Indian Movement, use "Indian" in their titles. Second, virtually all federal laws, such as the Indian Reorganization Act, and all federal agencies, such as the Bureau of Indian Affairs, use "Indian." Lastly, the term "Native Americans" includes Hawaiians, and this book does not address their legal rights, but only the rights of Indians and their tribes.

NOTE:

Alaska has over 200 Native Communities. Shown are the general locations of the Eskimos, Aleuts, and the Athabascan and Tlingit Indians.

Not all small groups in the lower 48 states are shown. Many Indians now live in urban areas such as Baltimore, New York City, Chicago, and Los Angeles.

0   100 200 300 400 500 miles

INDIAN LANDS AND COMMUNITIES

MALECITE
MICMAC
PASSAMAQUODDY
PENOBSCOT

NETT LAKE   GRAND PORTAGE
RED LAKE
LEECH LAKE   KEWEENAW BAY
RED CLIFF   BAD RIVER   OTTAWA AND CHIPPEWA
WHITE EARTH   BAY MILLS
FOND DU LAC
LAC COURTE   LAC DU
MILLE LAC   OREILLES   FLAMBEAU
ST CROIX   SOKAOGON
PRIOR LAKE   HANNAHVILLE
MENOMINEE   POTAWATOMI
GRANITE   PRAIRIE ISLAND   ONEIDA
FALLS   LOWER SIOUX   WINNEBAGO
STOCKBRIDGE   BROTHERTON
MUNSEE   ISABELLA
NEBAGO   POCAGON   POTAWATOMI
RA   POTAWATOMI

MOHAWK

ONEIDA
TONOWANDA   ONONDAGA
TUSCARORA
CAYUGA   SENECA   SCATICOOK
                    PAUGUSSET

NIPMUC
WAMPANOAG
PEQUOT
NARRAGANSET
MOHEGAN
MONTAUK
SHINNECOCK
POOSEPATUCK

SAC AND FOX

MIAMI

MOOR
NANTICOKE
RAPPAHANOCK
UPPER MATTAPONI
MATTAPONI
PAMUNKEY
CHICKAHOMINY
HALIWA

IOWA
SAC AND FOX
KAPOO
OMI
CHIPPEWA   WYANDOT
AND
UNSEE   SHAWNEE
ELAWARE   MIAMI
             PEORIA
             QUAPAW
OSAGE   SENECA CAYUGA
             WYANDOTTE
CHEROKEE
CREEK
SEMINOLE
CHOCTAW
CHICKASAW

AMHERST

CUBAN

CHEROKEE   COHARIE
            LUMBEE
CATAWBA   WACCAMAW

SUMMERVILLE

CHOCTAW

CHOCTAW
CHOCTAW   CHOCTAW   CREEK
            TUNICA
BAMA-COUSHATTA
        COUSHATTA
    CHITIMACHA
        HOUMA

SEMINOLE
        SEMINOLE
        SEMINOLE
        MICCOSUKEE
MICCOSUKEE

LEGEND

Dark Area - *FEDERAL INDIAN RESERVATIONS*
▲ - State Indian Reservations
■ - Other Indian Groups

0   100   200   300   400   500 miles
ALBERS EQUAL AREA PROJECTION

1971

1

A HISTORY OF FEDERAL INDIAN POLICY

More than 500 independent nations, and more than one million people, were prospering in what is now the United States when Europeans first arrived here. They lived in communities spread all across the land. Many of these communities were thousands of years old. All of the land in the United States was controlled by one nation or another. Today, few non-Indians in this country have any knowledge of the vast and highly developed civilizations that preceded them.

Most of the people centuries ago lived, as they do now, along the coasts, the major rivers, and the Great Lakes. Their societies were complex and specialized. There were Indian kings, doctors, artisans, architects, sculptors, mathematicians, religious leaders, and poets, to name just a few of their occupations. Every tribe learned how to live off its land: agricultural tribes developed irrigation systems, while tribes dependent on fish and game developed ways to catch, store, and preserve their food. Some communities built huge housing complexes, with gardens, living units, and courtyards. Nearly a thousand years ago, the

Anasazi Indians in the Southwest constructed a housing complex so large, it was not until 1882 that a bigger one was built, in New York City. In addition, many communities traded with one another, and trade networks spanned the continent.

When the Europeans arrived, most Indian tribes openly welcomed them, helped them, traded with them, and allowed them to live in their territory. Sadly for the Indians, they underestimated the Europeans and were too trusting. "What leaders of Indian nations did not understand, often until it was too late, was the way the Europeans viewed Indians. They were not white or Christian. They were savages—wild and brutish—in the minds of many."[1] Europeans were friends with the Indians when they needed to be, but when they were strong enough to overpower the Indians, they took full advantage of it.

By 1900, war and disease had reduced the population of Indians to three hundred thousand. Since 1900 the Indian population has increased to almost 2.5 million, nearly a third of whom are less than fifteen years old.

Indians live in every state in the United States. Nearly half of them live on or near Indian reservations. There are some 300 Indian reservations in the United States covering more than 52 million acres of land in 27 states. Reservations range in size from the 15.4 million-acre Navajo reservation (about the size of West Virginia) to the one-quarter-acre Golden Hill reservation in Connecticut. Most Indians live west of the Mississippi River, but 25 percent live in the Northeast, and North Carolina has the fifth-largest Indian population of any state.

Indians have the lowest life expectancy of any group in the country; as a whole, Indians live only two-thirds as long as the non-Indian population. Indians also suffer from a high rate of unemployment (which exceeds 70 percent on many reservations), and they fall well below the national average in income, quality of housing, and education (half the adult Indian population lacks a high-school diploma). "The red man continues to be the most poverty-stricken and economically deprived segment of our population, a people whose plight dwarfs the situation of any other Americans, even those in the worst big city ghettos."[2]

During the past ten years, more than 100 tribes have built gambling casinos on their reservations, some of which are highly profitable. On those reservations, economic conditions have improved. However, for the vast majority of reservation Indians, dramatic changes in the near future are unlikely, due to the many problems associated with reservation life, cultural differences, and persistent racial discrimination. In addition, most Indian reservations are located far from industrial centers and have no valuable natural resources, and thus remain dependent on government support for their economic survival.

A central problem that Indians face today is the complex and confusing pattern of federal laws that dominate their lives. No other ethnic or cultural group is so heavily regulated. These laws severely limit what tribes can do for themselves, both politically and economically.

The subject of this book is federal Indian law—the federal laws, regulations, court decisions, and policies that influence and control so much of Indian life. This subject can be understood more easily if it is placed in historical perspective.[3] First it must be recognized that there has never been a consistent federal Indian policy. On the contrary, federal policy with respect to Indians has shifted during the past 200 years from (1) regarding tribes as equals to the United States, (2) forcing tribes to move out of the East, (3) attempts to exterminate tribes or have them assimilate (join) into white society, and now (4) encouraging tribal independence. These policy changes have often been rapid and are usually highly disruptive, and Indians were almost never consulted in developing them. A brief summary of these policy shifts will help to place current Indian law in its context.

3

1492–1787: TRIBAL INDEPENDENCE

North America was "discovered" by Columbus in 1492. Columbus mistakenly thought that he had landed in the Indies and therefore the native peoples were called "Indians."

Europeans from a number of countries came to the New World, and the Indians allowed them to settle on their land. Treaties and agreements were made between the settlers and neighboring tribes in which European goods were exchanged for Indian land and assistance. These settlements could not have survived without the active support and protection of the Indians.

As these settlements grew in number, fights erupted over the control of land, especially between settlements occupied by different European countries. Invariably, each settlement attempted to enlist the support of nearby Indian tribes. A war known as the French and Indian War erupted in 1763 between English and French settlers. The Iroquois Confederacy,[4] the most powerful group of Indians north of Mexico, sided with the English. Had they chosen differently, people in the United States might speak French today.

1787–1828: AGREEMENTS BETWEEN EQUALS

In the years immediately following the Revolutionary War, the United States government regarded Indian tribes as having equal status with other nations, and every effort was made to keep their friendship. The United States was weakened after years of war with England, and it needed to avoid any war with an Indian tribe. Indian tribes were most concerned about protecting their land. Therefore, one of the first laws passed by Congress was aimed at assuring tribes that their land claims

4

would be honored and protected. This law, the Northwest Ordinance of 1787, declared: "The utmost good faith shall always be observed towards Indians; their land and property shall never be taken from them without their consent."[5]

Indeed, the First Congress passed a number of specific laws designed to protect Indians from non-Indians. In 1790 Congress required that persons who wished to trade with Indians must obtain a federal license, it authorized the prosecution of non-Indians who committed certain crimes against Indians, and it prohibited non-Indians from obtaining Indian land without the consent of the United States. In 1793, as a further sign of respect for Indian property, Congress prohibited non-Indians from settling on Indian lands.

Unfortunately, few of these laws were actively enforced, particularly those that might have discouraged settlers from moving westward. The government usually overlooked the forcible and illegal taking of Indian land. The federal government may have wanted to slow down westward expansion by white settlers, but it obviously did not want to prevent it altogether.

1828-1887: RELOCATION OF THE INDIANS

Federal Indian policy changed abruptly in 1828 when Andrew Jackson became president of the United States. Jackson was well known for his military campaigns against Indians. Under Jackson's administration, what previously had been an unspoken policy now became a publicly stated goal: removal of the eastern Indian tribes to the West. This removal policy remained as the federal government's primary Indian policy during the rest of the century.

The United States was now stronger, both economically

and militarily. It no longer needed to avoid hostility with the Indians; what the United States wanted most was Indian land. In 1830 Congress passed the Indian Removal Act, which authorized the president to "negotiate" with eastern tribes for their relocation west of the Mississippi River. Between 1832 and 1843, most eastern tribes either agreed to move to the West, or were forced to live on much smaller reservations in the East. Many eastern tribes were told that their new homes in Arkansas, Kansas, Iowa, Illinois, Missouri, or Wisconsin would be theirs permanently. However, the federal government broke almost every one of these treaties. Many tribes had to move several times farther west, each time being promised a permanent home.

The discovery of gold in California in 1848 brought thousands of settlers to the West and increased the desire for Indian land. Western tribes soon suffered the same fate as the eastern Indians: weakened by military campaigns, they were forced to accept reservation life and became increasingly dependent upon government rations for survival.

Congress passed a number of laws during the mid-nineteenth century in order to increase federal control over Indians and to promote the Indians being assimilated into white society. Particular emphasis was placed on "educating" and "civilizing" Indian youth. By 1887 more than 200 schools had been established under federal supervision, with an enrollment of over 14,000 Indian students, many of whom were forcibly removed from their families. The history of their authoritarian rule is notorious; for example, students were severely punished if they spoke their own language. In addition, Congress placed federal agents on Indian reservations in order to increase its supervision over Indian activities, and it authorized federal courts to prosecute Indians who committed certain crimes on the reservation.

Nearly a century after Congress passed the Northwest Ordinance in 1787, which acknowledged the independence and integrity of Indian tribes, Congress passed a law that reflects the degree to which the tribes' status had diminished. In 1871 Congress prohibited federal officials from making treaties with Indian tribes. Congress no longer considered Indian tribes as independent nations. From then on, Congress dealt with Indians by passing laws, which, unlike treaties, do not require tribal consent. If Congress wanted to take a tribe's land, all it had to do was pass a law to that effect. Many such laws were passed.

1887–1934: ALLOTMENT AND ASSIMILATION

In 1887 Congress passed the General Allotment Act, also known as the Dawes Act. The purpose of this act was to break up tribal governments, abolish Indian reservations, and force Indians to assimilate into white society. Under the act, individual Indians were assigned parcels of tribal land to own; for example, each head of household was assigned 160 acres of land. Many other portions of land were sold to non-Indian farmers and ranchers, who were being allowed to live on Indian reservations for the first time. Congress hoped that this process would not only break up tribal relationships but that, if whites settled on Indian reservations, Indians would learn and adopt white ways.

The effect of the General Allotment Act on Indians was catastrophic. Most Indians did not want to abandon their communal society and become farmers or ranchers. Besides, much of the tribal land was unsuitable for small-scale agriculture. Thousands of impoverished Indians sold their parcels of land to white settlers or lost their land in foreclosures when they were unable to pay state real estate taxes. In addition, tribal governments were seriously disrupted by the sudden presence of so many non-Indians on the reservation and by the huge decrease in the tribe's land base. Of the 140 million acres of land that tribes collectively owned in 1887, less than 50 million acres remained in 1934, when the General Allotment Act was repealed.

In 1924 Congress passed a law conferring U.S. citizenship on all Indians born in the United States. However, obtaining citizenship did little to improve the many economic and political problems that Indians faced.

1934–1953: INDIAN REORGANIZATION

In the early 1930s, federal Indian policy abruptly changed, and a more humane and considerate approach was adopted. A number of factors precipitated the change. For one thing, the onset of the Great Depression all but eliminated the desire and the ability of whites to purchase additional Indian lands. It also had become widely recognized that the General Allotment Act was very harmful to the Indians, disrupting their reservations, their culture, and their well-being. Mounting public criticism of the federal government's Indian policies encouraged President Franklin D. Roosevelt to make some radical changes.

In 1933 John Collier was appointed by Roosevelt as commissioner of Indian Affairs. Collier, who had long criticized the federal government's harmful Indian policies, declared in 1934: "No interference with Indian religious life or expression will hereafter be tolerated. The cultural history of Indians is in all respects to be considered equal to that of any non-Indian group."[6]

In June 1934 Congress passed the Indian Reorganization Act (IRA), also known as the Wheeler-Howard Act. The express purpose of the IRA was "to rehabilitate the Indian's economic life and to give him a chance to develop the initiative destroyed by a century of oppression and paternalism."[7]

The IRA prohibited the further assignment by the federal government of tribal land to individual Indians, and the sale of tribal land to non-Indians, without the tribe's consent. It also authorized the secretary of the interior to add lands to existing reservations, and to create new reservations for tribes that had lost their lands. Indian tribes were encouraged to adopt their own constitutions, to become federally chartered corporations, and to assert their inherent powers of self-government. The act established a $10 million revolving credit fund from which loans could be made to tribes. Finally, the act required that Indians be given a preference in employment within the Bureau of Indian Affairs, the agency that administers most of the federal government's Indian programs. Today, most BIA employees are Indian.

Between 1935 and 1953, Indian landholdings increased by over two million acres, and federal funds were spent for on-reservation health facilities, irrigation systems, roads, homes, and community schools. Unfortunately, the onset of World War II diverted the federal government's attention to other problems, and Indian economic well-being once again began to decline.

1953–1968: TERMINATION

During the 1950s Congress made another abrupt change in policy, abandoning the goals of the Indian Reorganization Act and ending its efforts to improve conditions on Indian reservations. The new policy Congress adopted brought Indian tribes to the brink of economic collapse. This new policy was called "termination": the termination of federal benefits and support services

9

to certain Indian tribes and the destruction of their reservations.

Between 1953 and 1962, Congress terminated its assistance to 109 tribes. Each of these tribes was ordered to distribute its land and property to its members and to dissolve its government. The tribe could no longer exercise any governmental powers, and all of its property was taken away. The tribe was essentially being forced into political extinction.

In an effort to reduce federal responsibility even further, Congress passed Public Law 83-280,[8] generally known as P.L. 280. This law gave six states complete criminal jurisdiction over Indian reservations, allowing them to enter the reservation to arrest Indians, remove them from the reservation, and try them in state courts. These six states (Alaska, California, Minnesota, Nebraska, Oregon, and Wisconsin) have large Indian populations. Previously, the federal government exercised criminal jurisdiction on Indian reservations in these states. Given that most Indian tribes do not get along well with state governments, this shift to state control was not in the best interests of Indian tribes.

1968-THE PRESENT: TRIBAL SELF-DETERMINATION

In 1968 President Johnson declared: "We must affirm the rights of the first Americans to remain Indians while exercising their rights as Americans. We must affirm their rights to freedom of choice and self-determination."[9]

Federal Indian policy thus shifted its course once again. President Nixon, who had been vice president during the termination era, expressly denounced the termination policy in 1970 and stated: "This, then, must be the goal of any new national policy toward the Indian people: to strengthen the Indian sense of autonomy without threatening his sense of community."[10] Similarly, in 1983 President Reagan reaffirmed the federal government's policy of promoting tribal self-determination: "This administration intends to restore tribal governments to their rightful place among governments of this nation and to enable tribal governments, along with State and local governments, to resume control over their own affairs."[11]

Since the late 1960s, Congress has passed a number of laws that promote Indian self-determination and economic development. An Indian Business Development Fund was created by Congress to stimulate Indian business and employment. Loan programs were created to lend money to tribes for the development of their natural resources. The Indian Self-Determination and Education Assistance Act of 1975, an historic piece of legislation, requires federal agencies to turn over various federal Indian programs to the tribes themselves, giving the tribes the same money the agency would have spent on the programs. Many tribes have used this opportunity to run their own health, education, and social services programs, giving them not only more control of their lives but also ridding themselves of unnecessary federal domination. The Indian Mineral Development Act of 1982 gives tribes the flexibility to enter into joint-venture agreements with mineral developers in order to maximize the tribes' financial return from their mineral resources. The Indian Gaming Regulatory Act of 1988 authorizes Indian tribes to engage in gaming, such as bingo and casino gambling, to raise money and promote economic development.

THE FUTURE

The future of federal Indian policy is impossible to predict. During the past 60 years alone, Congress has radically altered its Indian policies three times.

11

In recent years Indian tribes have increasingly asserted their treaty and statutory rights. Such activity is bitterly opposed by certain non-Indian groups, some of which are aggressively seeking the enactment of federal laws abolishing Indian and tribal rights. For example, owners of gambling businesses in Nevada and New Jersey, sensing competition from tribal casinos, are pouring money into lobbying efforts in Congress, requesting the passage of laws that would restrict tribal operations.

The next several years will be critical ones. In 1996, the Republican-dominated Congress cut a number of Indian programs in its effort to reduce the overall federal budget. For example, a program that provided $30 million to help Indian schools was eliminated. Other cuts have been threatened for the years ahead. These cutbacks would have such devastating effects that the assistant secretary of Indian Affairs, the person in charge of the Bureau of Indian Affairs, has accused Congress of entering another era of termination. In a newspaper editorial, the assistant secretary, Ada Deer, has stated that these cutbacks, if enacted, will violate the promises made to tribes in numerous treaties. "This country's first Americans," she writes, "deserve better treatment. They deserve honesty, candor and respect. The United States, at the very least, should keep its promises."[12]

2

DEFINITIONS: "INDIAN," "INDIAN TRIBE," "INDIAN COUNTRY," AND "INDIAN TITLE"

"INDIAN"

Who is an "Indian"?

Let's say that one of your four grandparents is 100 percent Indian, and the other three have no Indian blood. If that were true, then one of your parents is one-half Indian, and you are one-quarter Indian. Does that make you an Indian or a non-Indian?

Well, it depends. There is no single definition of the term "Indian."

Each Indian tribe, for example, has the right to decide for itself who can become a tribal member. Most tribes accept those people who have one-quarter or more tribal blood. Some tribes require less than one-quarter. In other words, you can have only a little Indian blood and still be a member of an Indian tribe, and thus be considered an Indian by your tribe.

The federal government has created hundreds of programs just for Indians—including housing, medical, and education programs—and each program uses its own definition of "Indian."

13

Many programs use one-quarter Indian blood as the standard. Other programs are open to anyone who is a member of an Indian tribe. As a result of these different standards, the same person might be an Indian in one situation but not in another.

Having these different standards can be confusing. The U.S. Census Bureau takes a simple approach when it prepares the census every ten years. The bureau lists every person as an Indian who claims to be one.

In short, there are many definitions of "Indian." Whether you are an Indian depends on many factors, including how much Indian blood you have, whether you want to be considered an Indian, whether you are accepted by the community or tribe as being an Indian, or whether you meet some government standard.

Are the native people of Alaska considered Indians?

The native people of Alaska comprise three groups: Eskimos, Aleuts, and American Indians. Eskimos and Aleuts constitute the majority of Alaska's native population.

Eskimos and Aleuts are a different race than the American Indian. Therefore, it is not correct to say that the native population of Alaska is Indians. However, it is true that Congress has made most federal Indian programs equally available to the Eskimos and Aleuts of Alaska. In that sense, there is no difference among these native groups.

Can someone be a citizen of both the United States and an Indian tribe?

Yes. In 1924 Congress declared that all Indians born in the United States are U.S. citizens. Indians do not lose their U.S. citizenship when they become a member of an American Indian tribe.

"INDIAN TRIBE"

What is an "Indian tribe"?

As with the term "Indian," the term "Indian tribe" has more than one definition. For example, ethnologists (experts who study cultures) define an Indian tribe as a group of Indians who share a common heritage and speak a unique language. Using this definition, there are more than 400 Indian tribes in the lower 48 states, and more than 200 Indian, Eskimo, or Aleut villages in Alaska.

The legal definition, however, varies. The federal government has established a list of standards that a group must meet to become a "federally recognized" Indian tribe. As a result of these standards, the federal government has refused to recognize more than 100 Indian tribes. This refusal has caused great controversy and bitterness.

A group of Indians can call itself a tribe and be recognized as one by other tribes, whether it is federally recognized or not. However, it cannot participate in the many programs that Congress makes available to federally recognized tribes if the group does not meet the federal standards. These programs include housing, health, social services, economic development, and education. Federal recognition is therefore extremely important to a tribe's survival and prosperity.

During the 1800s, the federal government sometimes placed two or more tribes on the same reservation, and these tribes today are treated as one tribe politically. An example is the Fort Belknap Indian Community in Montana, which is viewed as one tribe politically but is composed of two different tribes, the Gros Ventre and Assiniboine.

Also in the past, the federal government divided a tribe and placed those divided parts on different reservations. Today, many of these groups are federally recognized as separate tribes. Among these divided tribes are the Sioux, Chippewa, and Shoshone. For example, Sioux Indians were placed on nine reservations in South Dakota, each one of which is recognized today as a separate tribe by the federal government.

Is an Indian "nation" different from an Indian "tribe"?

The terms "nation" and "tribe" have been used interchangeably in federal Indian treaties and federal laws. However, the term "nation" usually refers to a government independent from any other government, having complete power over its land and people. Under this definition, Indian tribes are no longer nations because their power has been limited by the United States government and they do not have complete power over their land and people.

Some tribal governments, such as the Navajo Nation, continue to call themselves "nations" rather than "tribes." Many people believe that the United States has no right to limit the power of Indian tribes or control what they do, and that Indian tribes should be regarded as nations. This subject is discussed in chapter 5.

"INDIAN COUNTRY"

"Indian country" is one of the most important concepts in Indian law. It helps answer many questions concerning which government—tribal, state, or federal—has authority ("jurisdiction") in a particular situation.

As a general rule, the tribe and the federal government control the activities of Indians in Indian country, and not the state. For example, Indians who live and work in Indian country do not have to pay state income taxes, but they do have to pay tribal and federal taxes. Also, if they want to get a divorce, they would go to tribal court rather than state court. Most crimes by (or against) Indians within Indian country are governed by tribal or federal and not state law, and the state would have no jurisdiction over child custody or contract disputes involving Indians. Thus, a great deal depends on whether an area is part of Indian country.

The term "Indian country" was defined in a federal law first passed by Congress in 1790 (and modified slightly since then). This law is complicated, but basically, Indian country includes the following two geographic areas. First, *all* land within an Indian reservation is Indian country. That includes land owned by a non-Indian, as well as a highway owned by the state or federal government.

Second, Indian country includes land located outside an Indian reservation if the land has been set aside by the federal government primarily for the use and benefit of an Indian or tribe. The Pueblos of New Mexico, whose lands are owned by the tribes themselves but are under federal supervision, is an excellent example. Other examples include tribal housing projects located on federal land and federal schools operated for Indian children on federal land.

Are non-Indians permitted to live within Indian country?

Yes. Many non-Indians live within Indian country. (As explained in chapter 1, the federal government sold a large amount of reservation land to non-Indians between 1887 and 1934.) More non-Indians live on some Indian reservations than Indians. As an example, only 20 percent of the population of the Flathead Indian Reservation in Montana is Indian. Nevertheless, the entire reservation is Indian country.

What is an Indian reservation?

An Indian reservation is land that has been set aside by the federal government for the use, possession, and benefit of an Indian tribe or group of Indians. Most reservations were created by Congress, either through a treaty with a tribe or by passing a law creating a reservation. However, several reservations were created by the president of the United States by issuing an executive order. (The president can no longer create an executive order reservation because Congress passed a law taking away this power. Now, only Congress can create an Indian reservation.)

The terms "Indian reservation" and "Indian country" are not the same. As explained earlier, all land within a reservation is Indian country, but even land located outside a reservation can be Indian country. Thus, an Indian reservation is always Indian country, but Indian country includes more than Indian reservations.

"INDIAN TITLE"

What is "Indian title"?

The United States gained its independence from England after the Revolutionary War in 1781. At that time, most of the land in what is now the United States was still occupied and controlled by Indian tribes. Who owned all of this land: the tribes or the United States?

The U.S. Supreme Court—the highest court in the country —answered that question in 1823 in *Johnson v. McIntosh*. The Court held that the United States government had become the owner of all this land by virtue of the European "discovery" of the North American continent and the "conquest" of its inhabitants. It did not matter to the Court, apparently, that Europeans were not the first to discover North America—in fact, over 500 independent nations had been living here for centuries—and certainly had not conquered all the Indians. Many people believe that the Court reached its decision—that the United States owned all the land—because any other decision would have been very unpopular and probably impossible to enforce. Although popular among non-Indians, this decision has also been severely criticized on the grounds that it ignores the basic rights of native peoples.

The Court said in the same case, though, that each tribe retained a "right of occupancy" in its homelands. This right is known as "Indian title." As a result of Indian title, Indians have a right to remain on their homelands until Congress decides to take this land for another purpose. Thus, Indian title is "second best": the federal government owns this land, but the Indians have a right to live on it until Congress decides otherwise. Indian title includes the right not only to occupy the land but also to use its natural resources, such as water, timber, minerals, and fish and other wildlife.

There are two types of Indian title: "aboriginal" and "recognized." The latter carries an important legal right that the former does not: the right to compensation if this right is taken away. In other words, both types of Indian title can be removed ("extinguished") by Congress, but if the title is recognized, Congress must compensate the tribe for it, based on what the land is worth at the time it is taken.

Indian title becomes "recognized" only when Congress takes some formal action, such as signing a treaty or passing a law, that gives the tribe a right to permanent possession of the land. If Congress then takes away the land, it has to pay compensation to the tribe. The Just Compensation Clause of the Fifth Amendment to the Constitution provides that the government must pay compensation whenever it takes private property for some public use. (For example, if Congress takes your land so it can build an airport on it, it would have to pay you what the land is worth.)

Today, most tribes have been assigned to reservations, and the treaties or laws creating these reservations state that the tribes have a permanent right to stay there. Consequently, any taking of the land by Congress requires compensation to the tribe. As explained in chapter 4, Congress signed hundreds of treaties with tribes promising them permanent reservations, but Congress later broke almost all of these treaties and took the land. In reality, the promise of a "permanent" reservation means only that Congress can take the land anytime it wants to but it has to pay compensation.

Can the courts reverse a congressional decision to extinguish Indian title?

No. In 1941 the Supreme Court held that, under the U.S. Constitution, Congress has final authority concerning extinguishment of Indian title. If Congress decides to take from a tribe land that was promised in a treaty, a court cannot reverse that decision. A court can only ensure that fair compensation is paid. Only Congress, though, has this power. Neither the president nor any other branch of federal or state government can extinguish Indian title.

3

THE TRUST RESPONSIBILITY

What is "the doctrine of trust responsibility"?

Say that you own 150 acres of land, and the federal government wants to build an army base on it. The government makes you a promise: If you move to a much smaller home about 1,000 miles away, and you must walk to get there, the government will make sure that you will be safe and secure there. You agree to move. Does the government then have a duty to keep its promise?

This is the kind of question many tribes have been asking for a long time. Between 1787 and 1871, the United States entered into hundreds of treaties with Indian tribes. In almost all of these treaties, the Indians gave up land in exchange for promises. These promises included a guarantee that the United States would create a permanent home for the tribe (usually much smaller, and hundreds of miles away) and would protect the safety and future well-being of tribal members.

The Supreme Court has held that such promises create a "trust relationship" between the United States and the tribe, a "duty of protection" toward the Indians;[1] the United States must fulfill the promises that were given to the Indians in exchange for their land. The federal government's duty to honor this relationship and to keep its promises is known as its trust responsibility. This "doctrine" of trust responsibility is one of the most important principles in Indian law.

The Supreme Court recently confirmed "the undisputed existence of a general trust relationship between the United States and the Indian people."[2] The Court has used such terms as "solemn" and "special" to describe this relationship.

The Supreme Court first recognized the doctrine of trust responsibility in an 1831 case. However, for the next 100 years, the federal government (including the courts) did little to help tribes. To the contrary, the government broke almost every one of its Indian treaties. It also took the majority of land that tribes had been promised, killed thousands of Indians in wars the government started, and tried to destroy entire tribes and their reservations.

It is only during the past 60 years, and especially the past 30, that the doctrine of trust responsibility has become a positive force for Indians. Congress, as discussed in chapter 1, passed many laws during these years to help tribes improve their economies and become more politically independent.

In theory, the trust responsibility imposes broad obligations on the federal government. The government should remain loyal to the Indians and promote their best interests, including their interest in self-government. The federal government should encourage tribal independence, both economically and politically. In 1977 a Senate commission expressed this obligation as follows:

The purpose behind the trust doctrine is and always has been to ensure the survival and welfare of Indian

*tribes and people. This includes an obligation to pro-
vide those services required to protect and enhance
Indian lands, resources, and self-government, and
also includes those economic and social programs
which are necessary to raise the standard of living
and social well-being of the Indian people to a level
comparable to the non-Indian society.*[3]

However, as just explained, this theory has not always been
the government's practice, and recent events have caused Indians to once again worry whether Congress will remain faithful to
its trust obligations. In 1995 Congress began making huge cuts
in the federal budget. In the process, Congress reduced many
federal Indian programs, and eliminated a number of others.
These cutbacks are inconsistent with the trust responsibility.

Does the United States have a trust relationship with
every Indian tribe?

A broad interpretation of the federal government's trust
responsibility would recognize a trust relationship with every
Indian tribe. However, the Department of the Interior, which
administers most of the federal government's Indian programs,
has given the trust doctrine a narrow interpretation. The
Department of the Interior believes, for instance, that only
those tribes that have been officially "recognized" by the
department have a trust relationship with the United States. As
a result, the more than 100 tribes that have not met the department's tough standards cannot participate in federal programs.
As explained later in this chapter, the fault lies mainly with
Congress, which has the final authority regarding how federal
agencies operate. If Congress wanted to, it could order the
department to replace its narrow interpretation of the trust
doctrine with a broader one.

Does the trust doctrine apply to individual Indians?

Yes. The trust responsibility extends not only to tribes but also to their members. Theoretically, it extends to all tribal members, whether they live on or off the reservation. However, Congress has made few of the government's Indian programs available to off-reservation Indians.

Does the trust responsibility apply to off-reservation activities that could harm reservation Indians?

Yes. The federal government has a duty to protect Indians and tribes. Therefore, Indians can complain if the government engages in an activity outside the reservation that is harmful to Indians living on it. Using the trust doctrine, tribes have been able to stop federal agencies, for example, from using so much water outside the reservation that on-reservation water supplies are threatened, and from undertaking an off-reservation activity that would pollute the reservation.

Can Congress terminate a trust relationship?

Yes. Congress can end its trust relationship with an Indian tribe at any time, with or without the tribe's approval.[4] Between 1953 and 1968, Congress ended its trust relationship with more than 100 tribes. In each case Congress passed a law that terminated the tribe itself. Termination laws forbid a tribe from exercising governmental powers, require distribution of the tribe's property to tribal members, and end the tribe's trust relationship with the United States. The reasons why Congress has terminated Indian tribes are discussed in chapter 5.

Which federal agencies have the power to terminate a trust relationship?

None of them do. Once Congress has created a trust relationship with an Indian tribe, only Congress can end it. Even the tribe cannot terminate the relationship. Therefore, a federal agency must fulfill its trust obligations unless Congress orders it to stop.

Similarly, states have no power to terminate a tribe's trust relationship with the United States. Thus, a state's decision to provide services to an Indian tribe does not diminish the federal government's trust obligations.

Does it help a tribe to have a trust relationship with the United States?

Yes. Tribes that have a trust relationship with the United States are eligible to participate in many federal Indian programs. Most of these programs are available *only* to tribes that have a trust relationship with the federal government. These programs offer assistance in such areas as housing, health care, land development, social services, education, and employment. For example, the federal government provides millions of dollars to tribes for houses, roads, and sewers; it provides free medical care to reservation Indians; and it offers job assistance and educational scholarships to Indians.

Are there disadvantages to having a trust relationship with the United States?

Few tribes could survive economically without financial help from Congress. Therefore, having a trust relationship is very important to tribes because this qualifies the tribe to receive financial assistance from Congress. However, there are "strings" attached to this money. Thus, there are both advantages and disadvantages to having a trust relationship.

Congress has placed tribal land, money, and natural resources under the control of federal agencies. The primary agency is the Bureau of Indian Affairs, located within the Department of the Interior. In order for a tribe to develop its land, for example, or sell its oil, it must get an agency's permission. According to the trust doctrine, these federal agencies are supposed to help tribes, and Congress should make sure that they do. Unfortunately, these agencies have often hurt tribes by making bad decisions about the use of tribal property, and Congress has failed to stop them.[5] These agencies have also been reluctant to loosen their control over tribes and to give them much freedom and independence. In 1977, a U.S. Senate committee had this to say about the behavior of the Bureau of Indian Affairs:

> *The Bureau of Indian Affairs . . . has used the trust doctrine as a means to develop a paternalistic control over the day-to-day affairs of Indian tribes and individuals. Federal-Indian trust law, as expressed by both Congress and the courts, calls for Federal protection, not Federal domination. . . . The relationship should be thought of not only in the terms of a moral and legal duty, but also as a partnership agreement to insure that Indian tribes have available to them the tools and resources to survive as distinct political and cultural groups.[6]*

Thus, as tribes see it, there are two problems here. First, federal agencies have too much control over Indian government and property. Second, these agencies often make bad decisions with respect to both. Numerous studies and court investigations have found that federal agencies often mismanage Indian property and Indian programs. One such study, conducted by the *Arizona Republic* in 1987, concluded that the Bureau of Indian Affairs (BIA) "has failed to fulfill its responsibility as trustee for Indian holdings and as the designated protector of Indian rights," and it has been "costly, ineffective and unresponsive" to Indian needs. The BIA "actually has thrived on the failure of Indian programs . . . [and] deterred development" of Indian self-government. Specifically cited in the report were massive failures in employment, housing, education, and health-care programs; mismanagement of tribal timber, mineral, and oil and gas resources; and ineffective law enforcement.[7]

The fault lies primarily with Congress. Congress has the ultimate responsibility to fulfill this nation's treaty commitments, and to help tribes become independent. Yet Congress has broken nearly all of its Indian treaties, terminated more than 100 tribes, and Indians as a group are the most disadvantaged and impoverished in our society. In addition, Congress is supposed to oversee the operation of federal agencies to make sure they are helping tribes, not hurting them, but Congress often ignores this duty.

To be sure, Congress has passed many laws benefitting Indians, and it continues to provide Indians and tribes with numerous special programs and services. But overall, Congress has failed to provide tribes with the means to meet their basic governmental, economic, and social needs, contrary to its trust responsibilities. Likewise, federal agencies and agency officials are often of great assistance to Indians and tribes. But overall, their performance has been poor.[8]

Can the federal government's trust responsibilities be enforced by the courts?

Yes, if they are being violated by a federal agency. No, if they are being violated by Congress.

Few treaties require that Congress provide specific services, such as health care, housing, employment, or education. Therefore, Congress is not obligated to provide these services and cannot be forced by a court to do so. With respect to Congress, then, the trust responsibility is more of a moral than a legal obligation. If Congress decides to terminate its services

27

to an Indian tribe—or even to terminate the tribe itself—a federal court has no authority to prevent it. Indians, in other words, must rely on the good faith of Congress to keep the promises it made more than a century ago in exchange for Indian land.

However, once Congress creates a federal program and orders an agency to administer it in a certain way, tribes can go to court if the agency violates that duty. Likewise, a federal agency must not take any action that would violate the terms of a treaty between Congress and an Indian tribe. For instance, a federal agency cannot build a dam on land reserved by treaty to an Indian tribe unless Congress has expressly approved it. Congress has the authority to modify a trust relationship, but administrative agencies do not.

Federal officials must perform their trust duties with a high degree of care and responsibility. Indians have been successful in court, for example, in preventing federal officials from selling tribal land, from diverting water from their reservations, and from mismanaging tribal resources. Tribes have also obtained money damages for injuries to their property caused by agency mismanagement. In one case, a tribe recovered substantial damages when it proved that the BIA had mismanaged the sale of tribal oil and gas. In another case, a tribe recovered damages when it proved that the BIA had mismanaged the sale of the tribe's timber resources. All of these actions were based on the doctrine of trust responsibility.

4

INDIAN TREATIES

A treaty is an agreement between independent nations. The
Constitution authorizes the president, with the consent of two-
thirds of the Senate, to enter into a treaty on behalf of the
United States.[1] The Constitution declares that treaties are
"the supreme law of the land."[2] Therefore, they are superior to
state laws and state constitutions and are equal in authority to
laws passed by Congress.

A treaty can cover nearly any subject. The United States
has signed hundreds of treaties with other countries, involving
such subjects as trade, fishing on the high seas, travel, rules of
war, and the use of nuclear energy.

Until 1871, treaties were the accepted method by which the
United States reached agreements with Indian tribes. Nearly
every tribe has at least one treaty with the United States.

Is an Indian treaty a grant of rights to a tribe?

No. The Supreme Court has explained that an Indian treaty is
"not a grant of rights to the Indians, but a grant of rights from

them."[3] The purpose of an Indian treaty was not to give rights to the Indians but to remove rights that they had. Thus, Indians have a great many rights in addition to those listed in treaties. In fact, any right not expressly taken away by a treaty or federal law is "reserved" to the tribe. This fundamental principle of Indian law is known as the "reserved rights doctrine."

To illustrate, suppose that a treaty creates a reservation for a tribe to live on, but the treaty says nothing about the tribe having the right to hunt and fish on the reservation. Based on the reserved rights doctrine, the tribe would only have to show that it used to hunt and fish, prior to the treaty. Once it proved this, the tribe would retain its hunting and fishing rights because nothing in the treaty removed those rights.

Did Indian tribes enter into treaties voluntarily?

Before the War of 1812, the United States and the Indian tribes negotiated treaties as equals. The new nation, weakened from years of war with Great Britain, would have been no match for the Indians. Consequently, the early Indian treaties were voluntary and mutually helpful. The United States got land and peace from the Indians. In exchange, the United States gave goods and services to the Indians and promised to protect them from people on the frontier who might try to take their land.

The War of 1812 removed the last major threat of European intervention in U.S. internal affairs. Now that the United States was stronger and able to focus its military power on the Indians, friendship with them became less important. The population of the United States was growing, and people were moving into territory reserved for the Indians. Armed conflict was the result. Indian treaties after the War of 1812 rarely were voluntary.

The Creeks and Cherokees, who lived in the southeastern United States, suffered some of the first losses. In 1814 the

Creeks were forced to surrender 23 million acres of land to the federal government. In 1835 President Andrew Jackson forced the Cherokees to sign the Treaty of New Echota, in which they gave up all of their land east of the Mississippi River in exchange for land in the Oklahoma Territory. (After the treaty was signed, the federal government ordered the Cherokees to march some 2,000 miles to Oklahoma, on a journey which came to be known as the Trail of Tears; many Indians died.)

In the decades that followed, white settlers and prospectors moved westward by the thousands, and the U.S. Cavalry went along to protect them. One by one, the government defeated the Indian tribes, forced them to sign treaties, and placed them on reservations. These reservations were often hundreds of miles from their original homelands.

What do Indian treaties contain?

Nearly every Indian treaty contains at least two provisions. First, the Indians agreed to give land to the United States. Second, the United States promised to create a federally protected reservation, usually in another location, for them. Some treaties also promised the Indians specific goods or services, such as medical care, food and clothing, farm equipment, or cattle. (As discussed previously, the purpose of an Indian treaty was to take rights away from Indians; treaties rarely listed the many rights reserved to them, such as hunting, fishing, and water rights.)

Almost every treaty assured the Indians that they could live on their reservation permanently and would not be forced to move. In 1854 Senator Sam Houston described the perpetual nature of these reservations in the following terms: "As long as water flows, or grass grows upon the earth, or the sun rises to show your pathway, or you kindle your camp fires, so long shall you be protected by this Government, and never again be

31

removed from your present habitations."[4] Only rarely did the United States live up to these kinds of promises.

Does the United States still make treaties with Indian tribes?

No. In 1871 Congress passed a law that prohibited the making of treaties with Indians. This law (Title 25, United States Code, Section 71) declared that Indian tribes were not independent nations with whom the United States could make treaties. Since 1871 Congress has regulated Indian affairs through legislation. This makes it much easier for Congress. If Congress, for example, wants to take land from the Indians that is reserved by a treaty, all it has to do is pass a law, taking the land. The tribe's consent is not necessary, as it would be if a new treaty had to be signed. Congress has passed many such laws.

Did section 71 repeal the earlier Indian treaties? If not, are all of these treaties valid today?

Section 71 states that "no obligation of any treaty . . . shall be hereby invalidated or impaired." Thus, section 71 did not affect any existing Indian treaty. This does not mean, however, that every Indian treaty is still valid. In fact, most treaties have been abrogated (broken) by Congress. In 1903, the Supreme Court held in *Lone Wolf v. Hitchcock* that Indian treaties have the same authority as federal laws, but no greater authority. Therefore, a federal law can amend or repeal an earlier Indian treaty. In *Lone Wolf*, for example, Congress had signed a treaty with the Kiowa tribe promising never to place another tribe on its reservation. Some years later, Congress passed a law placing another tribe on the Kiowa's reservation. The Kiowas asked the Supreme Court to enforce the treaty, but the Court held that Congress had the right to pass these kinds of laws, abrogating Indian treaties. Since then, Congress has passed many

similar laws. The *Lone Wolf* decision has been severely criticized because it permits Congress to break a treaty whenever
it wants to.

The Fifth Amendment to the Constitution contains the Just
Compensation Clause, which guarantees that Congress will
not deprive anyone of "private property . . . without just compensation." The Supreme Court has held that Indian treaty
rights are a form of private property protected by this clause.
Consequently, Indians must receive fair compensation whenever Congress abrogates their treaty rights—including their
rights to live on their land and use the natural resources it contains—based on the fair market value of the property being
taken. The Kiowas in *Lone Wolf* were entitled to compensation
for the land they lost, but that is not what they wanted.

Money often provides little satisfaction to people who have
lost their homes or sacred lands, especially when they were
promised by the government that they could keep those homes
and lands forever. In a recent case, the Supreme Court awarded the Sioux more than $100 million in compensation for the
loss of the Black Hills in South Dakota. Immediately afterward,
a number of Sioux filed a lawsuit demanding that the federal
government keep the money and return the land. The court
refused to interfere with Congress's power to take the tribe's
land.

How are Indian treaties interpreted?

Many disputes have arisen over the terms and provisions of
Indian treaties. These disputes often involve important and
valuable interests in land, water, minerals, and wildlife.

The Supreme Court has developed a set of rules that govern
the interpretation of Indian treaties. These rules are known as
the "canons of treaty construction." There are three basic canons.
First, any uncertainty in a treaty must be resolved in favor of the

Indians. Second, these treaties must be interpreted as the Indians would likely have wanted it at the time. Finally, Indian treaties must be interpreted liberally in favor of the Indians.

These canons obviously benefit the treaty tribe, as the Supreme Court intended. Tribes were at a significant disadvantage in the treaty-making process. For one thing, treaties were always negotiated and written in English and the Indians were not certain what they were signing. Also, most treaties were signed under threat of force and were fundamentally unfair. Consequently, Indians should receive the benefit of the doubt when questions arise.

These canons have been extremely important to Indians. Tribes in the Northwest have particularly benefited from them. All of these tribes have long depended on fishing for their livelihood. The treaties they signed recognize their right to fish but fail to say exactly how many fish they may catch or where they may fish. The Supreme Court has liberally interpreted these treaties in favor of the Indians. According to the Court, these treaties allow the Indians to catch up to 50 percent of the fish, and to fish at many locations that are now outside the boundaries of the reservation. This subject is discussed in more detail in chapter 11.

In short, an Indian treaty must be interpreted broadly to accomplish its purpose. For example, a treaty that creates a permanent reservation for a tribe is presumed to reserve enough water to make the reservation livable. This is true even if the treaty makes no reference to water rights.

Has the United States honored its treaty commitments?

Generally, no. The United States has broken nearly every one of its Indian treaties. Most of them were broken to obtain Indian land.

To illustrate, in 1851 the Sioux signed a treaty that guaranteed them a sizable reservation as a permanent home, including what is now the entire western half of South Dakota. However, the federal government allowed hundreds of non-Indians to settle on this land in violation of the treaty. After several battles, in 1868 the Sioux were forced to sign a treaty that drastically diminished the size of their reservation. Although this treaty took most of their land, it at least left the Sioux their sacred Black Hills and promised that no additional land would be taken from them. However, gold was found in the Black Hills in 1874, and in 1877 Congress passed a law that removed the Black Hills from the reservation. Even this was not the end. In 1889 Congress removed half of what remained and carved the rest into six separate reservations, dividing the Sioux among them. Resistance to this action ended quickly with the killing of scores of unarmed Sioux at Wounded Knee in 1890. Between 1904 and 1910, Congress removed additional lands from the six reservations. The Rosebud Sioux Reservation, for example, was reduced to one-fourth of its 1889 size.

What standards are used to determine whether Congress has abrogated a treaty?

Lone Wolf v. Hitchcock makes it easy for Congress to break its treaty promises because federal laws can now abrogate Indian treaties without the tribe's consent. However, the Supreme Court has also held that Indian treaties cannot be abrogated unless Congress's intent to do so is "clear and plain."[5] In other words, when courts must determine whether a federal law has abrogated a treaty, it must uphold the treaty unless Congress has clearly abrogated it. To illustrate, Congress has passed a law allowing states to determine where to dump hazardous wastes. One state chose to dump its waste on an Indian reservation, claiming that this law authorized its doing so. However, the reservation was created by a treaty, and a federal court stopped the state from using the reservation as a dumping ground because Congress had not expressly authorized the state to abrogate the treaty. While this rule has helped tribes in many situations, Congress has passed laws expressly abrogating in whole or in part most Indian treaties.

Treaty abrogation discredits the integrity of the United States. Tribes relinquished vast amounts of land in exchange for treaty promises, and they have a right to expect the United States to keep those promises. As the late Supreme Court Justice Hugo Black stated in criticizing the breaking of Indian treaties by the federal government, "Great nations, like great men, should keep their word."[6]

Can an administrative agency abrogate an Indian treaty?

No. A federal agency cannot abrogate an Indian treaty without specific congressional authority. This is true even if the agency has some general authority to undertake the activity in question. For example, the Army Corps of Engineers has the general authority to build dams for flood control, but it cannot build a dam on Indian treaty land without the express consent of Congress.

Can a state abrogate an Indian treaty? Can a tribe?

A state cannot amend or repeal Indian treaty rights, and neither can a tribe. Only Congress can.

How can treaty rights be enforced?

Indian treaties have the same force and effect as federal statutes. A violation of an Indian treaty is a violation of federal law.

Indians and tribes are entitled to enforcement of their treaty rights. If state or federal officials violate these rights, a lawsuit can be filed in federal court to stop them from continuing to do so. Treaty rights can also be raised as a defense to a criminal prosecution. For example, if a state makes it a crime to hunt deer in December, an Indian cannot be found guilty of violating this law if he or she has a treaty right to hunt in December.

5

FEDERAL POWER OVER INDIAN AFFAIRS

The United States gained its independence from Great Britain in the Revolutionary War, which ended in 1781. During this war, a few tribes helped the American colonists, while a few helped the British. Most of the tribes that knew about the war apparently believed it wouldn't matter who won, and did not get involved.

The Indians soon learned differently. After the war, the newly formed federal government claimed it had the right to control every Indian tribe. It even claimed to own all the land the Indians were living on. The Indians, on the other hand, were unwilling to give up their independence—and their land—merely because the colonists had defeated the British.

The attempt by the United States to impose its laws on tribes, and to take their land, caused bitterness and often led to war. One by one, however, Indian tribes lost their land, usually by military force, and were placed on reservations often hundreds of miles from their original homelands.

Many people continue to believe that Indian tribes have the

right to be independent, and that the federal government has no right to interfere in tribal affairs.[1] The federal government does not agree. For more than 200 years, the federal government has forced its laws on Indian tribes. It is unlikely that Indian tribes will ever again be totally independent, free from federal control.

THE SOURCE AND SCOPE OF FEDERAL POWER OVER INDIANS

What is the source of federal power over Indians?

The ultimate source of the federal government's power over Indians is its military strength. The old saying of "might makes right" controls the relationship between the federal government and Indian tribes. The United States, with its superior military power, determines what is "right" for Indian tribes.

Over the years, the Supreme Court has given four reasons why the United States has a legal right to regulate Indians and tribes. Two of these are based on clauses contained in the U.S. Constitution. The Commerce Clause (article I, section 8, clause 3) provides that "Congress shall have the Power . . . to regulate Commerce with foreign Nations, and among the several States, and with the Indian Tribes." The Treaty Clause (article II, section 2, clause 2) gives the president and the Senate the power to make treaties, including treaties with Indian tribes. The Supreme Court has stated that these clauses provide Congress with "all that is required" for complete control over Indian affairs.[2]

In addition, the Supreme Court has cited a principle in international law as a justification for federal control over Indians. This principle is that, by virtue of the European "discovery" of North America and the "conquest" of its inhabitants, the federal government is entitled to enforce its laws over all persons and property within the United States.[3]

Lastly, the Court has cited the doctrine of trust responsibility (discussed in chapter 3) as a source of federal power over Indians. According to this view the federal government has a right, as well as a duty, to regulate Indians for their own "protection." Although all four of these justifications have been used at one time or another, the Supreme Court in recent years has cited the Commerce Clause as the most important source of federal power over Indians.

Many Indians (and non-Indians) have criticized these justifications. They point out that the Commerce Clause merely appears to allow Congress to regulate trade with Indians, not dominate them. Likewise, the Treaty Clause merely appears to allow the federal government to sign treaties with tribes, not control them. There is nothing in the Constitution expressly authorizing Congress to regulate Indian tribes. Nevertheless, the federal government has consistently held that it has the right to dominate and regulate Indians and tribes.

What is the scope of federal power over Indian affairs, and are there any limits to it?

The Supreme Court has held that Congress has virtually unlimited power over all Indian tribes, their governments, their members, and their property. But the Court has also held that this power is not absolute. Congress cannot do something that would violate the U.S. Constitution. Two limitations that are particularly important to tribes are the Due Process Clause and the Just Compensation Clause, both of which are contained in the Fifth Amendment to the Constitution.[4] The Due Process Clause prohibits Congress from discriminating against Indians on account of race and requires that laws passed by Congress be fair and reasonable. However, courts have upheld many laws that seemed quite unfair and unreasonable to the Indians who challenged them.

The Just Compensation Clause requires the federal government to pay for any private property it takes away. For instance, when Congress creates a reservation for a tribe, it cannot then take away this land without having to pay the tribe for it. The amount paid must compensate not only for the value of the land but also for any natural resources found on or in the land, such as timber or oil. The Just Compensation Clause does not prevent Congress from taking the land, but it requires that a fair price be paid for it.

Another limitation on Congress, at least in theory, is the doctrine of trust responsibility. As explained in chapter 3, this doctrine obligates the federal government to remain loyal to Indians and tribes, to act in their best interests, and to fulfill treaty promises. However, Congress has often ignored its trust obligations and done many harmful things to tribes, such as take their land.

Why can Congress pass laws that give Indians special treatment?

Over the years, Congress has passed hundreds of laws that apply only to Indians. Some of these laws help Indians, while others hurt them. Federal laws, for example, provide Indians with educational, medical, financial, and housing benefits from the federal government that non-Indians are not eligible to receive. Other laws, however, place restrictions on Indians, especially in the use of their land, that non-Indians do not have.

All of these laws have one thing in common: they treat Indians differently from non-Indians. Yet the Constitution prohibits discrimination on the basis of race. So, how is this discrimination possible?

41

This discrimination is allowed, the Supreme Court has explained, because these laws are not "racial" laws. True, Indians are a different race than non-Indians, but this is not the reason Congress treats them differently. Congress treats them differently because they were here first, and both the colonists and, later, the United States entered into treaties with them. Race was not the issue. Indians are a separate political group —our native population. The Commerce Clause of the Constitution, as just explained, authorizes Congress to regulate commerce with the Indians. In addition, the federal government's trust responsibility requires it to help the Indians. Therefore, Congress can treat Indians differently from non-Indians and not engage in unlawful race discrimination.

A case that illustrates this principle is *Morton v. Mancari*, decided by the Supreme Court in 1974. In that case, the Court considered whether a law passed by Congress in 1934, the Indian Preference Act, constitutes unlawful race discrimination. The act requires that Indians receive a hiring preference for job vacancies within the Bureau of Indian Affairs (BIA). Non-Indians challenged this law, claiming that it discriminated against them on the basis of race. In a 9–0 decision, the Court upheld the law. The Preference Act, the Court found, was politically, and not racially, motivated: Congress passed this law in order make sure that Indians would be employed within the federal agency that most directly affects them, the BIA. Therefore, this law was a reasonable exercise of Congress's broad power over Indians.

Thus, each federal Indian law must be examined in its historical, political, and cultural context before deciding whether it constitutes illegal discrimination. If the law can be tied to the right of Congress to treat Indians as a separate political group, the law is a valid exercise of congressional power, even if it discriminates for or against Indians. To date, in fact, not a single federal law regarding Indians has been invalidated by the Supreme Court on the grounds that it constitutes race discrimination, even though Congress has passed hundreds of laws that treat Indians differently from non-Indians.

IMPLEMENTATION OF FEDERAL POWER

Congress has virtually unlimited authority to regulate Indians and tribes, including their form of government and their property. Congress can assist a tribe or destroy a tribe, and it has done both. We will now examine some of the ways that Congress has intervened in Indian affairs: administration of Indian affairs; regulating tribal governments; termination; regulating Indian land; regulating individual property; trade and liquor regulation; and criminal jurisdiction.

Administration of Indian Affairs

Who administers the federal government's Indian policies?

The Constitution divides the federal government into three branches: legislative, judicial, and executive. The legislative branch (Congress) makes the law. The judicial branch (the courts) interprets the law. The executive branch (whose chief officer is the president) administers the law.

The Commerce Clause assigns to Congress, and Congress alone, the power to create the federal government's policies regarding Indians and tribes. Congress creates these policies by passing laws. However, while only Congress can pass laws, these laws must then be administered by others. Most often, they are administered by a federal agency located within the executive branch of government, which means that the president, or persons under the president's command, hires and supervises the staff.

Congress has passed so many laws dealing with Indians, and created so many Indian programs, that nearly every aspect of Indian life falls under the control of some federal agency. Congress does not have the time to watch these federal agencies every day. Moreover, laws passed by Congress often give an agency broad authority to decide how something should be done. As a result, federal agencies have a great deal of leeway —and a great deal of power—in administering federal law.

The federal agency that administers most of the federal government's Indian programs is the Bureau of Indian Affairs (BIA). The BIA is located within the Department of the Interior. The assistant secretary of Indian Affairs is the highest-ranking official within the BIA and is appointed by the president subject to the Senate's approval. The assistant secretary reports to the secretary of the interior, who answers only to the president. Under the assistant secretary are thousands of BIA employees to help administer the government's Indian programs.

Although the BIA administers most of the federal government's Indian programs, other agencies oversee many Indian programs as well. The total budget for these programs currently exceeds one billion dollars. These other programs include medical care administered by the Department of Health and Human Services, food programs administered by the Department of Agriculture, and housing programs administered by the Department of Housing and Urban Development.

What powers have been delegated by Congress to the secretary of the interior?

Congress has created dozens of programs for Indians and has directed the secretary of the interior to manage most of them.

This is called "delegating" authority. For example, the secretary has been delegated the power to regulate the sale and lease of tribal land; operate social welfare programs on reservations; control the use of water on irrigated Indian lands; regulate and approve Indian wills; operate schools for Indian children on the reservation; and purchase land for Indians and tribes.

What powers have been delegated by Congress to the president?

The Constitution gives Congress the exclusive right to establish the federal government's Indian policies. Accordingly, the only power the president has over Indian affairs is what Congress has delegated to that office. Congress has not delegated any specific powers to the president regarding Indians. Of course, the president could greatly influence how Indian programs are administered, given that most of these programs are run by the secretary of the interior, who is under the president's command. However, few presidents have taken an active role in administering Indian programs.

During the late nineteenth century, several presidents began creating Indian reservations without the permission of Congress. These were called "Executive Order" reservations. Congress was so upset by this that it passed a law prohibiting the president from creating any more of them. In 1887, as explained in chapter 1, Congress authorized the president to take land from Indian tribes and assign the land to individual Indians. In 1934, Congress removed this power. At the present time, the president has no specific Indian affairs authority.

Can Congress delegate authority to Indian tribes?

Yes. Congress can delegate to Indian tribes the same powers it can delegate to a federal agency. In recent years, tribes have been authorized to administer many social welfare, health, and education programs formerly managed by federal agencies. Many tribes now operate their own school systems, irrigation projects, health-care, welfare, and food programs, receiving from Congress the same money that federal agencies had been getting to run these programs.

Have federal officials done a good job in their administration of Indian affairs?

Generally, no. Federal administration of Indian affairs has been soundly criticized. The BIA has the reputation in Washington as the worst-managed agency in the federal government.[5] A 1977 Senate committee report described it as inefficient, insensitive, and antagonistic to tribal self-government. In 1987, the assistant secretary of the interior, the officer in charge of the BIA, described his own agency as a public-administration disaster that should make radical changes in the way it treats Indians and manages Indian programs.[6] As evidence of the BIA's bad management, a recent study found that the BIA had failed to collect *eleven billion* dollars owed to tribes by oil companies.[7] For many years now, Indians, as well as members of Congress, have been calling for major reform of the BIA. However, the BIA has successfully resisted most efforts to make it more accountable to its Indian clients.

Regulating Tribal Governments

Congress regulates many, if not most, activities of tribal governments. Indian tribes cannot even lease their own land without having the BIA's approval. Indeed, virtually every decision tribes make concerning their land and other assets must be submitted for approval to a federal agency.

During the past 20 years, Congress has begun relaxing its

tight grip on tribal government. Congress has passed several laws, in fact, that give tribes substantial authority over reservation activities. These laws are discussed in chapter 1.

In a similar trend, federal courts are now taking a closer look at federal agency decisions that are opposed by an Indian tribe. In growing numbers, courts are requiring federal agencies to follow the wishes of the tribe when managing tribal property and other resources, unless the agency can prove that it has a compelling reason not to do so. In other words, federal courts are giving the doctrine of trust responsibility, discussed in chapter 3, broader application, and are requiring federal agencies to use their powers in the tribe's best interests and to allow tribes to make their own decisions more frequently.

Termination

What is "termination"?

Another way in which Congress regulates Indian affairs is by exercising its power of termination. Termination is the process by which Congress abolishes a tribe's government and ends (terminates) the federal government's trust relationship with that tribe. Congress can do nothing worse to an Indian tribe; termination is the ultimate weapon of Congress and the ultimate fear of tribes.

Between 1953 and 1968, Congress terminated 109 tribes, most of them in Oregon and California. In each case, Congress passed a law directing the secretary of the interior to distribute all of the tribe's property to tribal members. The tribe's reservation was then eliminated, and the tribe and its members became ineligible to receive the government services generally provided to Indians and tribes.

In addition to abolishing the tribe's government and reservation, termination also makes it difficult for Indians to main-

47

tain their cultural and religious heritage, which is usually tied to the land and their community. Despite its harmful effects, the Supreme Court has held that Congress has the power under the Commerce Clause to terminate a tribe.

Why has the federal government terminated Indian tribes?

There are a number of explanations. Some people claim that termination is in the best interests of Indians. Termination, they say, will help Indians integrate into white society, eventually raising their standard of living and reducing Indian poverty.

Many other people believe that Congress did not design termination to help Indians. They believe that Congress terminates tribes so that non-Indians can obtain Indian land and the federal government can save money by eliminating its treaty promises and trust responsibilities. As one Indian describes it, "The Congressional policy of termination . . . [is] a new weapon in the ancient battle for Indian land. . . . In practice, termination is used as a weapon against Indian people in a modern war of conquest."[8]

Has Congress halted its termination policy?

Yes, but the threat of termination is never far away. A bill introduced in Congress in 1977 called for the termination of every Indian tribe, but the bill did not pass. Congress has not terminated a tribe since 1966, and it has even restored to federal status several tribes it previously had terminated, returning to them land and benefits that had been taken away. In 1970 President Nixon stated that the "policy of forced termination is wrong" because the United States has "solemn obligations" owed to the Indians in exchange for taking their land. To end this relationship, the president said, "would be no more appropriate than to terminate the citizenship rights of any other American." Moreover, termination has proven to be "clearly harmful" to the tribes that were terminated and "has created a great deal of apprehension" among other tribes. He therefore urged Congress not to terminate any more tribes.[9]

Regulating Indian Land

Originally, all the land in the United States was controlled by Indian tribes. Over the years, the federal government took most of it from them by force or threat of force. Now, only some 50 million acres remain in tribal hands, only a small fraction of their original possessions, and much of this is barren desert.

All of this land is regulated by Congress. Congress justifies this regulation on the grounds that Indians need help in how to keep and use their land.

Indian land is either trust land or nontrust ("deeded") land. Trust land is owned by the federal government but set aside for the exclusive use of an Indian or tribe. Deeded land is owned outright by an Indian or tribe. Most Indian reservations consist entirely or mostly of trust land.

The Supreme Court has held that all Indian land, both trust and deeded, is subject to the control of Congress. Congress has placed many restrictions on the use and sale of Indian land.

What restrictions have been placed on the sale, lease, and inheritance of Indian trust land?

Congress has passed many laws governing the sale, lease, and inheritance of Indian trust land. The federal government controls everything that occurs on this land because the federal government owns it. Indians and tribes only have a "beneficial interest" in trust land—the right to use it.

Given that the United States owns all trust land, it cannot be sold by the "beneficial owner" (the Indian or tribe) unless the government agrees to issue a deed to the land. The secretary of the interior decides whether a deed should be issued, under guidelines set by Congress.

Similarly, Indians and tribes cannot lease their trust land to someone else unless the secretary of the interior consents to the lease. Laws passed by Congress create many different kinds of leases, such as grazing, mining, oil and gas, and residential leases. Congress has created a set of rules for each type of lease. For instance, a lease for grazing purposes cannot exceed a term of 10 years, while a lease for residential purposes may be made for 25 years. Any lease that does not comply with federal law is invalid. Usually, the secretary will consent to a lease when requested by the beneficial owner, provided that the terms of the lease comply with federal law.

Congress also regulates the inheritance of trust land. Indians who are the beneficial owners of trust land can transfer their interests when they die, but only in accordance with the rules set by Congress. For example, Congress has issued rules governing how Indians must write their wills in order to transfer their trust land.

What restrictions have been placed on the sale, lease, and inheritance of deeded Indian land?

As explained in chapter 1, from 1887 until 1934 many Indians were allotted parcels of trust land. (A head of household, for instance, received 160 acres.) Later, some of these Indian "allottees" were given deeds to their parcels. This removed the land from trust status and it became privately owned. Deeded land owned by an individual Indian can be sold by the Indian owner at any time.

Any Indian whose allotted land still remains in trust status can request that a deed be issued by the secretary of the interior. The secretary is required to issue the deed unless the Indian is found to be unable to manage the property. Once the deed is issued, the Indian becomes the owner of the land and can sell it whenever he or she wishes.

Many Indians feel that they should be able to obtain these deeds and sell their land whenever they want to. Unfortunately, the continued sale of trust land is harmful to tribal government because most of it is sold to non-Indians. In order to protect tribes, the secretary usually gives the tribe an opportunity to purchase the land from the Indian allottee before a deed is issued. This way, the tribe can buy it rather than allow it to be sold to someone else.

Deeded land owned by a tribe is treated differently by the federal government than if it were owned by an individual Indian. A federal statute enacted in 1790 prohibits tribes from selling their land, whether trust or deeded, without the approval of the federal government. Any sale of tribal land without the government's consent is void.

Congress has decided not to regulate the inheritance of deeded land. Therefore, Indians who own deeded land can transfer it when they die, just as non-Indians can.

Are there other ways in which Congress regulates trust land?

Yes. Besides controlling the sale, lease, and inheritance of trust land, federal laws also control rights-of-way on trust land. Under these laws, the secretary of the interior must consent to any highway, power line, or oil and gas pipeline that someone wants to place across trust land. The secretary also manages the timber grown on trust land, and thus the tribe must obtain the secretary's permission to sell any timber grown on this land.

Is it possible for an Indian or tribe to obtain additional trust land?

Congress has created two methods by which tribes and individual Indians can obtain additional trust land. Both methods require secretarial approval. First, the secretary can use federal funds and purchase deeded land, and then convert it into trust land. The secretary, however, cannot be forced to purchase land for any particular Indian or tribe. Some one million acres of land have been purchased for tribes under this program, but this is a relatively small amount given how much land the government took from tribes.

Second, an Indian or tribe can purchase deeded land and request that the secretary convert it into, or exchange it for, trust land. As explained later in this book, there are a number of tax and other advantages to having land in trust status. In 1988, for example, the secretary placed in trust status land owned by a tribe so that the tribe could conduct a bingo operation on it free from state regulation.

Can Congress diminish the size of, or abolish, an Indian reservation?

Yes. Congress has diminished the size of many reservations and abolished many others. The Supreme Court has upheld the right of Congress to do this provided that the government pays the tribe a fair price for any land that is lost. Methods that Congress has used to take land from tribes include (1) removing a tribe and placing it on a smaller reservation elsewhere (this was done to most of the eastern tribes), (2) decreasing the size of an existing reservation (this was done to most of the reservations in the West), (3) selling land within a reservation to non-Indians (this was done to most of the reservations in the country), and (4) terminating the tribe altogether and eliminating the reservation (which Congress did to 109 tribes). Each method results in more land being available for purchase by non-Indians, which is the main reason land is taken from tribes.

Are there any limitations on the federal government's control over Indian land?

The major limitation is the Just Compensation Clause, but it does not stop Congress from taking Indian land. It only guarantees that Congress will pay compensation for any land that is taken.

Regulating Individual Property

Does Congress regulate the private property of Indians?

Some property, yes; other property, no. In theory, Congress has the power to regulate all private property of Indians, including the wages earned from private employment, but it has not chosen to do so. Mainly, the only private property of Indians that the federal government regulates is trust land and money obtained from the use of trust land. For example, money received from the lease of an Indian's trust land, or from selling timber from that land, is deposited into that person's Individual Indian Money (IIM) account under the control of the secretary of the interior. Federal law requires that all money in an IIM account must be used for the "benefit" of the Indian.

These IIM accounts are controversial. In order for Indians to withdraw their money from them, they must convince some government official that it will be used for their "benefit." Some government officials make it difficult for Indians to withdraw these funds by imposing their own standards of how it should be spent. In addition, officials may be guilty of mismanagement. A lawsuit filed in 1996 alleges that some 300,000 Indians lost billions of dollars from their IIM accounts through government mismanagement and bad record-keeping.

Indian children can have IIM accounts also, which hold income they receive from any trust property they may have inherited. The secretary must manage these accounts in the best interests of the children. Even a child's parents cannot withdraw funds from these accounts unless they show the money will be used for the child's benefit.

Trade and Liquor Regulation

Does Congress have the power to regulate trade with the Indians?

Yes. The Commerce Clause gives Congress the express power to regulate commerce with the Indian tribes. There is almost no aspect of Indian trade that is not federally regulated. As early as 1790 Congress passed a comprehensive law to regulate trade with the Indian tribes, and most of its provisions are still in effect. This law requires all persons, except Indians "of the full blood," who trade on an Indian reservation to obtain a federal license and to obey certain restrictions on the type of goods and services being offered and the manner of their sale. Violators are subject to the forfeiture of their goods and a $500 fine.

Anyone who discovers that someone is violating these federal regulations is authorized by federal law to file a lawsuit against that person. If the court finds a violation, the trader's goods must be confiscated by the federal government and sold, and the informer is entitled to half the proceeds.

Does the government's power to regulate trade include the power to regulate the sale of liquor?

Yes, and Congress has extensively used this power. Initially, Congress prohibited all sales of liquor to Indians, both on and off the reservation. Congress then changed the law so that it applied only to sales on or near Indian reservations. Still later, Congress prohibited only on-reservation sales. Finally, Congress authorized each tribe to decide for itself what liquor regulations to establish, and to issue liquor licenses under its own rules. Some tribes, like the Navajo Nation, have banned all liquor on the reservation.

Criminal Jurisdiction

Congress has passed laws authorizing federal and state officials to prosecute Indians who commit certain crimes on the reservation. These laws represent another example of the federal government's desire to control Indians and tribes. The extent to which Congress exercises criminal jurisdiction in Indian country is explained in chapter 8.

6

TRIBAL SELF-GOVERNMENT

Indian tribes have the right to govern themselves. They had this right centuries before Europeans arrived on this continent, and they have it today.

The Supreme Court first recognized this "inherent right of tribal sovereignty"—the basic right of an Indian tribe to be independent and self-governing—in an 1832 case, *Worcester v. Georgia*. The issue in *Worcester* was whether the state of Georgia could enforce its laws on the Cherokee Indian Reservation, a reservation within the state. In holding that Georgia could not apply its laws on the reservation, the Court stated:

> *Indian nations [are] distinct political communities, having territorial boundaries, within which their authority is exclusive, and having a right to all the lands within those boundaries, which is not only acknowledged, but guaranteed by the United States. . . . The Cherokee nation, then, is a distinct community,*

> *occupying its own territory, with boundaries accurately described, in which the laws of Georgia can have no force, and the citizens of Georgia have no right to enter, but with the assent of the Cherokees themselves, or in conformity with treaties, and with the acts of Congress.*[1]

The *Worcester* rule of "inherent tribal sovereignty" has undergone some changes over the years, but its basic principles remain the same. Congress has the authority to limit or even abolish tribal powers, and thus tribes are "limited" sovereignties. But unless Congress limits a tribe's powers, the tribe retains its *inherent* right of self-government, and the state lacks the power to enforce its laws on the reservation.

THE SOURCE AND LIMITS OF TRIBAL POWER

What is the source of tribal power?

The source of a tribe's power is its people. Congress has the ability to limit tribal powers, but it did not create them. Indian tribes have the inherent right to govern themselves.

What are the limits of tribal power?

The Supreme Court has described Indian tribes as being limited sovereignties. That is, tribes have inherent powers, but Congress may limit (and even abolish) those powers. This is a principle of law, but more than that, it is a political reality. The federal government has the raw physical power to limit or abolish tribal governments. Over the years, Congress has abolished many tribal governments and limited the authority of the rest. The exercise of this power has been extensively criticized, as discussed in chapter 5.

Indian tribes have two types of limitations on their powers: express and implicit. Congress has expressly prohibited tribes from doing certain things, such as selling tribal land without the federal government's permission. These express limitations are discussed in the previous chapter. In addition, Indian tribes have implicitly lost certain powers. For instance, Indian tribes cannot enter into treaties with foreign governments, declare war, or coin money. According to the Supreme Court, tribes lost these powers due to their subordinate position as "conquered" and "dependent" nations. Yet despite these express and implied limitations, Indian tribes retain an enormous amount of power.

Tribal governments have a unique position in our society. No one word or phrase can accurately describe their status. It is often said that tribes have sovereign powers. However, tribes are not fully sovereign because Congress has supreme authority over them. Nevertheless, tribes are very powerful. In some situations, tribes can even do more than states can do, as will be explained later.

During the past 200 years, most tribes have been economically, culturally, and governmentally injured by the United States. As a result, few tribes have the ability to exercise all of their powers. Even those that do, use their powers cautiously. Thirty-five years ago, during the termination era discussed in chapter 1, Congress "rewarded" some of the more self-sufficient tribes by terminating their federal assistance, with disastrous results. Many non-Indians continue to urge Congress to decrease (if not eliminate) tribal powers, usually for their own political or economic reasons. (For instance, many off-reservation businesses do not like the competition that tribal businesses present.) Only time will tell how successful these efforts will be.

Are tribal powers limited by the U.S. Constitution?

No. A century ago, the Supreme Court held that the Constitution does not apply to the exercise of tribal powers because it was not intended to. The Constitution limits only the powers of the federal and state governments, the Court said.

The Constitution places Indian tribes under the control of Congress. Consequently, Congress can limit tribal powers, but tribal powers are not limited by the Constitution itself. This means that tribal governments can pass laws that, if passed by the federal or state governments, would violate the U.S. Constitution.

THE SCOPE OF TRIBAL POWERS

Tribal governments have the same powers as the federal and state governments to regulate their internal affairs, with a few exceptions. The remainder of this chapter examines the nine most important areas of tribal authority: (1) forming a government; (2) determining tribal membership; (3) regulating tribal property; (4) regulating individually owned property; (5) the right to tax; (6) the right to maintain law and order; (7) jurisdiction over non-Indians; (8) the right to regulate domestic relations; (9) the right to regulate commerce and trade.

Forming a Government

Does an Indian tribe have the right to form a government?

Yes. The right to form a government is the first element of sovereignty, the most basic right of any political community. Therefore, Indian tribes possess this right. Long before Europeans arrived on this continent, each tribe had a government.

The right to form a government includes the right to set qualifications for government office, to determine how these officials are chosen, and to define their powers. For example, a tribe can require that candidates for tribal office be members of the tribe and speak the tribe's language. Each tribe also has the right to determine who can vote in its elections.

What types of governments do Indian tribes have?

Tribal governments vary considerably. There are more than 400 Indian tribes in the United States, and probably no two tribal governments are the same. A few tribes, for example, are theocracies (religious leaders control the government). Some tribes determine their leaders by heredity, but most tribal officials are elected. Most tribes have written constitutions and laws, and their own court system to enforce them, while other tribes depend on state or federal agencies to maintain law and order on the reservation. Most tribes have a central government similar to that of the United States, but some do not. The Hopi tribe, for example, is a union of nine self-governing villages, and each village decides for itself how it shall be governed.

Under the Indian Reorganization Act of 1934[2] 181 tribes chose to restructure their governments, and they are known as IRA tribes. The IRA was intended to help tribes "modernize" their governments. Many tribes were ill-equipped to manage the type of governmental affairs associated with reservation life, such as the need to enter into business contracts, operate police departments and courts, manage private property, collect taxes, and borrow money. The 1934 act gave tribes two years to decide whether to become an IRA tribe.

The IRA allowed each tribe to draft a new constitution giving the tribe specific powers, subject to the approval of the secretary of the interior. The secretary was directed to approve constitutions that created a tribal council having the power to enter into contracts with federal, state, and local governments, employ legal counsel, and manage the tribe's property. The secretary encouraged tribes, in addition, to give their councils the power to borrow money on behalf of the tribe; to assess and collect taxes; to create a tribal court system and enact a law-and-order code; and to create agencies within the tribe for governmental, economic, or educational purposes. Most IRA tribes gave these powers to their councils.

The main drawback of the IRA was that it gave the secretary of the interior the power to review the tribe's constitution and laws. Many tribes feared the federal government. However, most tribes viewed the IRA as helpful. Those tribes that voted not to become an IRA tribe created their own style of government. Many non-IRA tribes, such as the Navajo Nation, created a government similar to those approved under the IRA, but it has more autonomy because it is not subject to the secretary's review. However, these non-IRA tribes are ineligible to receive federal loans created by the IRA.

Today, most tribal governments have the same three branches as the federal and state governments: a legislature (which makes the law), an executive branch (which administers the law), and a judicial branch (which interprets the law). These functions are performed, respectively, by the tribal council, the tribal chairperson, and the tribal court. But tribal governments are not required to have this "separation of powers," and many do not.

Are there conflicts within tribal governments?

Many tribes now have a government very different from their traditional form of government. Traditionally, leadership status went to individuals who excelled in certain skills, possessed great wisdom, practiced generosity, displayed great courage, or had great spiritual powers. Today, tribal leaders are chosen by new methods, often for different reasons than before, and govern under a different set of rules than did their ancestors. Moreover, some Indians have learned how to use these new governmental systems to their personal advantage.

These rapid changes in tribal government have produced tremendous conflict on some reservations. Deep divisions have developed in some tribes between "traditionals" and "moderns," as well as along economic, religious, or political lines. Bitter disputes have erupted. On many reservations, tribal members mistrust tribal officials and have accused them of corruption and misuse of power.

Indian tribes have the inherent right to form their own government and to change it as the need arises. The United States government, too, has undergone radical changes over the years. (Under the original U.S. Constitution, for example, women were denied the right to vote and African Americans were slaves.) Tribes must be allowed the same freedom to change their form of government to suit their current needs and goals.

Determining Tribal Membership

Does a tribe have the right to determine tribal membership?

Indian tribes have the inherent right to determine who can join the tribe. As the Supreme Court has noted, "A tribe's right to define its own membership for tribal purposes has long been recognized as central to its existence as an independent political community."[3]

Tribal authority over membership includes the power to take membership away from a person. It also includes the right to adopt persons into the tribe. As with all other tribal powers, Congress can limit a tribe's membership powers, but it has not done so. Each tribe thus enjoys the exclusive right to determine who qualifies for enrollment.

What are the qualifications for tribal membership?

Most tribes determine eligibility for membership by blood fraction ("blood quantum"). In most tribes any person who has at least one-fourth degree of tribal blood qualifies for membership. (Thus if you are one-fourth Navajo and marry a non-Indian, your children would be one-eighth Navajo, and therefore ineligible for membership in the Navajo Nation, which has a one-fourth blood quantum requirement.) Some tribes enroll persons having as little as one-thirty-second blood quantum.

A few tribes have other membership requirements. Some tribes require residence on the reservation for a certain length of time or residence at the time of application. Some require the filing of a membership application within a few years after the applicant's birth.

Can a person become a member of two Indian tribes?

Yes. If a person's parents are members of different tribes, that person may qualify for membership in, and the benefits of, both of them, depending on the rules of each tribe. Many tribes, though, will not enroll someone already enrolled in another tribe. Therefore, a person may have to disenroll from one tribe in order to enroll in another. The United States has a similar rule: a citizen of another country cannot become a U.S. citizen without relinquishing the first nationality.

Regulating Tribal Property

What kinds of property can tribes own?

Indian tribes can own the same kinds of property non-Indians can own: real property and personal property. Real property consists of land and items attached to or found within the land, such as buildings, timber, and minerals. Personal property consists of all other kinds of property, such as cattle, bank accounts, automobiles, furniture, clothing, and other movable property.

In addition, Indian tribes can have two property interests in land that non-Indians cannot have: tribal "trust" land and "Indian title" land. Tribal trust land is land that has been set aside for the exclusive use of a tribe but is owned by the United States. Many tribes have considerable amounts of trust land. Given that this land is owned by the federal government, it cannot be taxed by the state, which saves the tribes a lot of money. However, it also means that tribes must get the federal government's permission when they want to use or lease the land.

Indian title land is land that has always been a part of a tribe's ancestral homesite. A tribe has the right to continue living on this land until Congress removes its right to do so. This right of continued occupancy is known as Indian title. Indian title is explained more fully in chapter 2.

How have Indian tribes obtained their interests in land?

Most Indian reservations were created either by a treaty between the tribe and Congress, or after 1871 (when Congress no longer entered into Indian treaties) by a federal law passed by Congress. In addition, several Indian reservations were created by the president of the United States, a power that Congress eventually took away in 1927. Some tribes have increased the size of their reservations by purchasing private land.

A few tribes received land grants from foreign countries

prior to the time the United States became a nation, and the United States later agreed to honor these rights. The most notable example is the Pueblos of New Mexico. All nineteen Pueblos received land grants from Spain and Mexico before becoming part of the United States, and the United States agreed to honor these rights, allowing the Pueblos to own the land given them by these foreign countries.

To what extent can an Indian tribe protect its property by regulating reservation activities?

Congress may limit the right, but until it does, a tribe has the same authority to protect and regulate its property that other governments have. The Supreme Court reaffirmed the inherent right of a tribe to regulate on-reservation activities in *Merrion v. Jicarilla Apache Tribe* (1982). In *Merrion,* discussed more fully in chapter 10, the Court held that Indian tribes have the inherent right "to tribal self-government and territorial management."[4] As a result of this right, the Court said, Indian tribes have the authority to assess taxes on non-Indians using tribal lands.

Similar decisions have been made in other contexts. Courts have held, for example, that Indian tribes have the right to regulate hunting and fishing on the reservation, control alcoholic beverages on the reservation, eject trespassers from tribal lands, tax Indians and non-Indians who use tribal lands for farming, cattle grazing, or other purposes, and regulate commercial activities on the reservation.

Are there any limits on the tribe's power to regulate reservation activities?

Yes. Indian tribes have the inherent right to regulate reservation property. However, (1) Congress can limit this right, and (2) tribes have lost the right to regulate certain activities due to their "dependent" and "conquered" status. In other words, as explained earlier, tribes can have both *express* and *implied* limits on their powers.

Most of the *express* limits that Congress has placed on the right of tribes to regulate reservation activities involve the use of trust land and are discussed in chapter 5. Congress has placed few limits on tribes in such vital areas as taxation, domestic relations (marriage, divorce, child custody, etc.), commercial transactions, and hunting and fishing. In fact, Congress has helped tribes protect their property by making it a federal crime to trespass on tribal land in a manner that violates tribal law.

In addition to the (few) express limits on tribal powers, certain *implied* limits exist. For example, the Supreme Court has held that, due to the tribes' dependent status, they may not prosecute non-Indians who commit crimes on the reservation. (As explained in chapter 8, these non-Indian lawbreakers must be prosecuted instead by the state or federal government.) In general, though, all activities of Indians and non-Indians on the reservation that involve tribal land, or affect an important tribal interest, are within the tribe's power to regulate and control.

If a tribe sells tribal land in violation of federal restrictions, is the sale valid?

In 1790 Congress passed a law that forbids tribes to sell their land without the consent of the United States. This law still exists. Any sale of tribal land without the consent of the federal government is invalid and can be voided at any time—even decades later.

This law has received much attention in recent years because it appears that portions of Maine, Massachusetts, Connecticut, Rhode Island, and New York were purchased 200 years ago from Indian tribes without the federal government's consent and must either be returned to the tribes or purchased again. In 1980, Congress appropriated $81.5 million to settle lawsuits brought by tribes in Maine seeking to recover land sold in violation of this law. This money was used to purchase land from the tribes that Maine thought it had already purchased nearly 200 years ago, and also was used to purchase 305,000 acres of replacement land for the tribes.

What is communal property?

The importance of a land base to Indian tribes cannot be overemphasized. It provides not only a home and a place to earn a livelihood but, on most reservations, it is a unifying force and has religious significance as well.

Few Indian tribes believed in the private ownership of land. Any land controlled by the tribe belonged to the entire community, and each member had the same right to use it as every other member. This concept of land ownership, known as communal property, was a guiding principle of Indian life and culture: land could not be privately owned, which meant that members of the community had to work together to harvest or gather what they could from the land. Anglo-American values, in contrast, tend to support the private ownership of property and the accumulation of individual wealth.

As explained in the previous chapter, in 1887 Congress passed the General Allotment Act, under which parcels of reservation land were taken from tribes and given to tribal members or sold to non-Indians. It was hoped by Congress that, by breaking up communal property, this would eventually cause Indians to assimilate into (join) white society. Once Indians learned how to support themselves as private landholders, Congress thought, they would no longer need tribal governments, and their reservations could be eliminated.

The General Allotment Act was a dismal failure, for reasons

67

previously explained. The act was repealed in 1934, but by then tribes had lost two-thirds of their land, and many non-Indians were living on Indian reservations.

Regulating Individually Owned Property

Does the tribe have the right to regulate private property within the reservation?

Every sovereign nation must place certain restrictions on the use of private property in order to protect the safety and welfare of its citizens and resources. Indian tribes retain the inherent right to exercise these powers unless Congress has limited that right or tribes have lost it due to their dependent status.

Indian tribes have broad authority to regulate private property. Congress has placed few restrictions on this authority. For example, courts have upheld the right of tribes to regulate the sale of liquor on the reservation, even from land owned by a non-Indian; to determine who may inherit private property belonging to a deceased tribal member; to take private land for tribal use (the power of eminent domain); and to impose health, safety, and employment regulations on businesses within the reservation, including those owned by non-Indians.

There are two exceptions to the general rule that tribes can regulate private property on the reservation. Both exceptions concern land privately owned by non-Indians. The Supreme Court has held that Indian tribes cannot regulate non-Indian hunting and fishing on non-Indian land, or regulate how a non-Indian uses privately owned land located in an area of the reservation that is primarily non-Indian owned, unless the non-Indian's activity threatens the safety, health, or economic well-being of tribal members. For example, a non-Indian who owns land on an Indian reservation can hunt deer on the property in violation of tribal hunting laws, unless he or she begins taking so many deer it threatens tribal food supplies.

As important as these exceptions are—and as damaging to tribal sovereignty—they remain exceptions. In most circumstances, tribes can regulate all privately owned land within the reservation.

The Right to Tax

The right to tax is an essential instrument of government. Only by collecting taxes can a government acquire enough money to manage its affairs and provide services to its citizens. Indian tribes must be allowed the same authority to tax that state governments have in order to become truly self-governing, reduce their dependence on federal aid, and provide a full range of municipal services to their members. Chapter 10 explains that, except in rare situations, tribes can tax both Indians and non-Indians on the reservation. As the Supreme Court stated in a 1982 case: "The power to tax is an essential attribute of Indian sovereignty because it is a necessary instrument of self-government and territorial management."[5]

The Right to Maintain Law and Order

No government can long survive without the power to maintain law and order. Every nation has the inherent right to make its own criminal laws and enforce them.

Chapter 8 discusses in detail the right of tribes to maintain law and order on the reservation. To briefly summarize, tribes have the inherent right to enact criminal laws, retain their own police force, create tribal courts and jails, and punish *Indians* who violate tribal law. However, in *Oliphant v. Suquamish Indian Tribe* (1978), the Supreme Court held that tribes, due to their dependent status, have lost the right to prosecute *non-*

Indians. Chapter 8 discusses the difficulties this lack of authority causes Indian tribes.

What restrictions has Congress placed on tribal law enforcement?

As in all other areas of tribal power, Congress may limit the right of tribes to engage in law enforcement. In 1968 Congress passed a law that places several such limits. This law, the Indian Civil Rights Act (ICRA), limits the penalties that tribes can impose to one-year imprisonment and a $5,000 fine. In addition, this act requires tribal courts to extend certain rights and to follow certain procedures in criminal trials. These rights and procedures are discussed in chapter 14.

What types of court systems do tribes have?

Indian tribes had their own systems of law and order long before Europeans arrived in North America. These differed greatly from the ones brought over by the Europeans. In particular, tribes handled misbehavior primarily through public scorn, the loss of tribal privileges, or the payment of restitution to an injured party, rather than by imprisonment. In the more extreme cases, banishment from the tribe might occur, and in some tribes an Indian family might avenge the death or injury of one of its members.

Congress has required tribes to abandon certain traditions, but not all of them. As just explained, the ICRA requires Indian tribes to use certain procedures, and to provide certain rights, in criminal cases. As a result, today most tribal courts closely resemble their non-Indian counterparts, the state and federal courts.

Tribal courts are quickly learning to apply a set of laws and procedures unknown to them until recently. Although tribal courts operate on various levels of what some people might call "professionalism," they are effective and comprehensive. The constitution of the Blackfeet tribe of Montana, for example, creates a small-claims court, a traffic court, a juvenile court, a court of general civil and criminal jurisdiction, and an appellate court containing five judges. The Navajo Nation probably has the most sophisticated judicial system; its courts process over 45,000 cases a year.

Each tribe sets its own qualifications for tribal judge, and these vary from tribe to tribe. Some tribes require that judges be tribal members. Some tribes require that judges be state-licensed attorneys. Some tribes elect their judges, but most appoint them. Each tribe also decides who is eligible to appear as an attorney or advocate in tribal court. Indian courts in general are evolving institutions that will require breathing room and tolerance until their role in Indian life and culture becomes firmly established, and each tribe develops the system that works best for that tribe.

Jurisdiction Over Non-Indians

Can Indian tribes regulate the activities of non-Indians on the reservation?

Initially, reservations were reserved exclusively for Indians. Today, thousands of non-Indians live on Indian reservations, especially as a result of the General Allotment Act (which opened most reservations to settlement by non-Indians). Thousands more work on or travel through Indian reservations each day. Thus the extent to which tribes have jurisdiction over non-Indians has important consequences.

As indicated earlier, non-Indians are generally subject to the full range of tribal law, except that they cannot be criminally prosecuted by the tribe. Tribes do, though, have an important power over non-Indians that helps compensate for the lack of criminal jurisdiction: the power to exclude. Indian

71

tribes have the inherent right to determine who can enter their reservations and under what conditions they can stay. As the Supreme Court stated in 1983: "A tribe's power to exclude nonmembers entirely or to condition their presence on the reservation is . . . well established."[6] Thus, tribes may at least remove non-Indian lawbreakers from the reservation, even though they cannot prosecute or imprison them. In addition, if non-Indians are violating state or federal law, tribal officials can arrest them and turn them over to state or federal officials.

Although tribes have the inherent power to exclude, they have been cautious about using it because Congress has the authority to limit that right. It would not be wise, for example, for a tribe to suddenly remove all non-Indians from its reservation because this probably would prompt Congress to limit the exclusion power.

The Right to Regulate Domestic Relations

Does a tribe have the right to regulate the domestic relations of its members?

Domestic relations include marriage, divorce, adoptions, and similar matters relating to home and family life. Regulation of domestic relations is an integral aspect of sovereignty. The inherent right of an Indian tribe to regulate the domestic relations of its members is well recognized. As the Supreme Court stated in 1978, "Unless limited by treaty or statute, a tribe has the power . . . to regulate domestic relations among tribe members."[7]

Congress has the ability to limit these tribal powers, but it has not done so. Thus, tribes possess not only the inherent authority but also the exclusive authority to regulate the domestic relations of its members within the reservation. For example, in a 1976 case, the Supreme Court decided that only tribal courts could determine the custody of a reservation Indian child whose parents were getting a divorce, and that state courts had no authority in such cases.

Do Indian tribes still rely on Indian custom to determine the validity of marriages, divorces, and adoptions?

Some do and some do not. Indian custom remains important on most reservations, particularly in the area of domestic relations. The central role of the family, the respect given to elders, the assistance that extended family members give to raising the children of relatives, and the overall importance of kinship have unique significance in Indian life.

Nevertheless, many Indian customs have changed over the years, as customs have in all cultures, especially when one culture is surrounded by another. For example, some tribes require their members to comply with state laws concerning marriage, divorce, and adoption, such as obtaining a state marriage license. Other tribes issue their own marriage licenses, and their tribal courts issue divorce decrees. A few tribes have passed laws forbidding marriage, divorce, or adoption by Indian custom, while other tribes continue to recognize them. In some tribes, a divorce was accomplished by placing the other person's belongings outside the home, which signified that the relationship was over.

If an Indian couple is married under state law, can they be divorced in a tribal court?

Yes. Any court can divorce couples who were married elsewhere, provided that the legislature has given the court this power. People married in Colorado can obtain a divorce in Nevada if they meet Nevada's requirements for divorce. Similarly, Indians married under state law can be divorced in a tribal court if they meet the tribe's requirements.

73

The Right to Regulate Commerce and Trade

Does an Indian tribe have the right to regulate commerce and trade within the reservation?

Yes. An Indian tribe has the same essential authority as any sovereign government to regulate economic activity within its territory. This includes the power to tax business activities and regulate the use of property within the reservation, whether owned by an Indian or a non-Indian. The few exceptions to this power were discussed earlier in this chapter.

As with all other tribal powers, Congress may limit the tribe's right to regulate commerce and trade. Congress has given federal officials considerable regulatory authority in this area, including the right to require every person other than a full-blooded Indian to obtain a federal license to trade on the reservation. However, these regulatory powers generally do not limit tribal powers. Rather, they impose federal regulations in addition to those that the tribe may impose. Although tribes may not pass any laws that conflict with federal regulations, they are not prevented from regulating the same activity. For example, people who sell goods on an Indian reservation can be required to purchase both a federal and a tribal trader's license.

Do Indian tribes have the right to engage in commerce and trade?

Certainly. An Indian tribe has the inherent right to engage in business activities as well as to create and license business corporations. Many tribes own their own businesses, including craft industries; mining, fishing, and gambling operations; ski resorts, motels, and restaurants. Congress has passed a number of laws, discussed in chapter 1, to assist tribes in their economic development.

Most Indian reservations are located far from urban and industrial centers. Thus they often find it difficult to attract industry, and poverty is rampant. On many reservations, unemployment exceeds 70 percent. Given these problems, it is vitally important that the federal government make a strenuous effort to improve economic conditions on the reservation. Alternatives include giving tax incentives to businesses willing to locate on an Indian reservation, and assisting tribes in marketing their products. The federal government has spent billions of dollars subsidizing farmers, tobacco growers, the dairy and airline industries, and a host of other special interests. It seems only fair that the government should also assist tribes in making their reservations economically viable.

Other Rights of Indian Tribes

Indian tribes have numerous other rights besides those covered in this chapter. These rights are discussed elsewhere in this book. For instance, chapter 4 discusses Indian treaty rights. Tribal rights under the doctrine of trust responsibility are discussed in chapter 3. Chapter 11 discusses hunting, fishing, trapping, and gathering rights, and chapter 12 discusses water rights.

7

STATE POWER OVER INDIAN AFFAIRS

Every Indian reservation is located within the boundaries of a state. This is a fact that many state and tribal officials wish they could change.

States have the right to regulate all persons and activities within their borders, with one major exception. The U.S. Constitution gives Congress exclusive authority over certain subjects, and one of these is Indian affairs.[1] Therefore, as a general rule, a state is not allowed to apply its laws within an Indian reservation unless Congress has authorized it to do so. Congress has given the states very little authority to regulate reservation Indians. As the Supreme Court has noted, "The policy of leaving Indians free from state jurisdiction and control is deeply rooted in the Nation's history."[2]

States and tribes are not often friends. States dislike the fact that reservation Indians usually cannot be taxed or regulated by the state, and Indians dislike the states' constant attempts to find ways to tax and regulate them. The state-Indian conflict has been a long and bitter one. Many states and tribes are now working hard to improve their relations with one another, for their mutual benefit. Hopefully, the future will see continued efforts in this direction.

STATE JURISDICTION OVER RESERVATION INDIANS

Do states have the right to regulate the activities of reservation Indians?

As a general rule, no.

In an early case, *Worcester v. Georgia* (1832), the Supreme Court held that state laws cannot be enforced on an Indian reservation unless Congress has authorized the state to apply them there. Since then, the Supreme Court has relaxed this rule. Today, certain kinds of state laws can be applied within Indian country even if not authorized by Congress. However, it is still the general rule that states cannot regulate the activities of reservation Indians without the express consent of Congress.

Can Congress give rights to Indians without the state's consent?

Yes. As explained in chapter 5, the U.S. Constitution gives Congress final authority over Indian affairs. Federal Indian treaties and statutes do not need state approval before becoming the "supreme law of the land." When Congress decides to do something for Indians within a state, it does not need the state's approval.

CONGRESSIONAL AUTHORIZATION OF STATE JURISDICTION

State laws cannot be applied in Indian country, as a general rule, unless authorized by Congress. Knowing this, states often pressure Congress for permission to regulate reservation activities. States are rarely successful in this effort. However, during the past 200 years, Congress has passed three laws that have significantly increased state jurisdiction over reservation life.

The General Allotment Act of 1887

How did the General Allotment Act increase state jurisdiction in Indian country?

The General Allotment Act of 1887[3] has been discussed in earlier chapters. This act was extremely harmful to Indians. By the time it was repealed in 1934, tribes had lost almost two-thirds of the lands they held in 1887, and life on most reservations was changed forever.

Basically, the Allotment Act authorized federal officials to decide whether an Indian reservation contained any "surplus" land. If it did, this land could be sold by the federal government to non-Indians. In addition, the act authorized federal officials to take land away from the tribe, divide the land into parcels, and give tribal members deeds to these parcels. Once the deed was issued, the land could be sold. Many parcels of land were then sold to non-Indians.

Three major things happened as a result of the General Allotment Act. First, tribes lost the majority of their land. Ninety million acres of tribal land were sold to non-Indians, leaving tribes with less than 50 million acres. Second, the presence of so many non-Indians living on the reservation disrupted the traditional life of the tribe. Third, the act gave extra money to the states. States can tax privately owned land on Indian reservations. Therefore, states could now tax this 90 million acres of privately owned reservation land, resulting in millions of dollars of new tax revenues.

Public Law 83-280

As explained in chapter 1, the years between 1953 and 1968 are known as the "termination era" in federal Indian history. During this period, Congress tried to destroy certain Indian tribes, force Indians to fully join ("assimilate") into white culture, and reduce the government's assistance to Indians.

Public Law 83-280[4] (often written as "P.L. 280" or "Pub. L. 280") was passed by Congress on August 15, 1953. (It is reprinted in appendix B.) It was designed to reduce federal expenditures to tribes and encourage the assimilation of Indians into white culture, by giving the states greater power on Indian reservations. "Without question," the Supreme Court said in 1979, P.L. 280 reflects "the general assimilationist policy followed by Congress from the early 1950s through the late 1960s."[5]

How did P.L. 280 increase state jurisdiction in Indian country?

Public Law 280 gives to five states complete criminal jurisdiction over Indian reservations located within the state. These five states were required to apply all of their criminal laws on the reservation, thereby making Indians subject to the same criminal laws as everyone else in the state. These states had no choice but to accept this jurisdiction and are therefore known as the "mandatory" states. The five mandatory states are California, Minnesota, Nebraska, Oregon, and Wisconsin. In 1958 Alaska was added by Congress as a sixth mandatory state.

P.L. 280 authorized the other 44 states, at their option, to assume the same jurisdiction the mandatory states had received. These states are known as the "option" states. Of the 44 option states, only 10 took steps to accept any jurisdiction under P.L. 280. The jurisdiction these states took is illustrated in a table later in this chapter.

What is "partial" jurisdiction?

Public Law 280 does not expressly authorize an option state to accept anything less than the full jurisdiction given to the mandatory states. However, most option states that assumed any jurisdiction assumed only partial jurisdiction. These states limited their jurisdiction to (1) less than all the Indian reservations in the state, (2) less than all the geographic areas within an Indian reservation, or (3) less than all subject matters of the law. For instance, Montana only assumed criminal jurisdiction on the Flathead Indian Reservation, one of seven reservations in the state. Arizona assumed jurisdiction only with respect to the control of air and water pollution. In 1979 the Supreme Court held that it was legal under P.L. 280 for an option state to assume only partial jurisdiction, even though this created a "checkerboard" situation in which some portions of the reservation and not others, and some crimes and not others, were subject to state jurisdiction.

Which reservations within the six mandatory states are under P.L. 280 state jurisdiction?

Within the six mandatory states, all Indian reservations except for three are under P.L. 280 jurisdiction, as shown in the table below.

State	Extent of Jurisdiction
Alaska	All Indian country within the state.
California	All Indian country within the state.
Minnesota	All Indian country within the state, except the Red Lake Reservation.
Nebraska	All Indian country within the state.
Oregon	All Indian country within the state, except the Warm Springs Reservation.

| Wisconsin | All Indian country within the state, except the Menominee Reservation. |

Which reservations within the option states are under P.L. 280 state jurisdiction?

Ten option states accepted jurisdiction under P.L. 280. Only Florida accepted the full jurisdiction given the mandatory states. The other nine took partial jurisdiction. Jurisdiction within the option states is shown below.

State	**Extent of Jurisdiction**
Arizona	All Indian country within the state, limited to enforcement of the state's air and water pollution control laws.
Florida	All Indian country within the state.
Idaho	All Indian country within the state, limited to the following subject matters: compulsory school attendance; juvenile delinquency and youth rehabilitation; dependent, neglected, and abused children; mental illness; domestic relations; operation of motor vehicles on public roads.
Iowa	Only over the Sac and Fox Indian Community in Tama County, limited to civil and some criminal jurisdiction.
Montana	Over the Flathead Reservation, limited to criminal jurisdiction and later, by tribal consent, to certain domestic relations issues.

State	Extent of Jurisdiction
Nevada	Over the Ely Indian Colony, and any other reservation that may subsequently consent.
North Dakota	Limited to civil jurisdiction over any reservation that gives its consent. No tribe has consented.
South Dakota	A federal court invalidated the jurisdiction assumed by the state and therefore no P.L. 280 jurisdiction exists.
Utah	All Indian country within the state with tribal consent. No tribe has consented.
Washington	All privately owned land within Indian country. Jurisdiction on trust land is limited to certain subjects, such as operating motor vehicles and juvenile delinquency. These tribes have requested and are now under full state criminal jurisdiction: Chehalis, Colville, Muckleshoot, and Nisqually.

In what way was Public Law 83-280 changed in 1968?

Most Indian tribes strongly opposed P.L. 280 at the time of its passage. Afterward, tribes continued to worry because option states could increase their jurisdiction over them at any time. In response to these concerns, Congress amended P.L. 280 in two respects in 1968. First, Congress placed a tribal-consent requirement in the law. A state can no longer obtain any P.L. 280 jurisdiction over a tribe unless a majority of the tribe's members vote to give its consent. Second, the 1968 amendments authorize the United States to accept a "retrocession" (a return) of any jurisdiction that a state received under P.L. 280. In other words, a state can give back to the federal government any jurisdiction it has under P.L. 280. Indian tribes, though, cannot force a state to gave back its jurisdiction, and even when a state does offer to retrocede, the United States is not required to accept that offer.

Since 1968, several states have retroceded jurisdiction. For example, in 1975 Nevada retroceded jurisdiction over all but one of its tribes (the Ely Indian Colony).

Termination Laws

In addition to the General Allotment Act of 1887 and Public Law 83-280, Congress has used one other means to greatly increase state jurisdiction over Indians. This third method, termination, is the most devastating to Indian interests of the three.

The process of termination and its effects are explained in chapters 1 and 5. Between 1953 and 1968 Congress passed laws that terminated 109 tribes. Basically, each of these laws required the affected tribe to distribute all of its property to its members and to disband its government. The tribe ceased to exist as a governmental body, and its members became fully subject to state law. As a result of these termination laws, thousands of Indians and millions of acres of Indian land came under state jurisdiction.

Other Congressional Authorizations of State Jurisdiction

Congress has passed several laws that confer state jurisdiction over particular tribes. Oklahoma and New York, for example, have been given some jurisdiction that most other states do not have over the Indian tribes in those states.

Congress also has conferred state jurisdiction over particular subjects. For example, Congress has authorized the secretary of the interior to allow state officials to inspect reservation health conditions and enforce the state's sanitation and quarantine laws on Indian reservations. States have also been authorized to tax oil, gas, and other minerals produced from certain Indian lands and to regulate the sale of liquor on Indian reservations.

Thus, every state has some jurisdiction on Indian reservations. Few states, however, have much authority. This is particularly true in the vital areas of domestic relations (marriage, divorce, adoptions, child custody, etc.), commercial transactions, taxation, and land use, where Indians are involved. For the most part, Congress has kept tribes and reservation Indians free from state jurisdiction. This is somewhat surprising, given that states have pressured Congress for more than 200 years to increase their jurisdiction over Indians and tribes.

STATE JURISDICTION WITHOUT CONGRESSIONAL AUTHORIZATION

From the earliest days of the republic, states have attempted to extend their laws into Indian reservations. When Congress refused to authorize these extensions, states then tried to control reservation activities even without congressional approval.

Occasionally, states have gotten away with it. In 1881, for instance, the Supreme Court held that a state could prosecute a non-Indian for killing another non-Indian on an Indian reservation. In 1885 the Court held that a state could tax the personal property of a non-Indian that was located on an Indian reservation. These cases held for the first time that a state could regulate certain reservation activities without the consent of Congress.

The Supreme Court has now developed a two-part test to determine which state laws can be enforced in Indian country without congressional consent: the federal preemption test and the infringement test. A state law must pass both tests in order to be valid. Moreover, state laws affecting reservation activities must be viewed against a "backdrop" of tribal sovereignty, the *inherent* right of an Indian tribe to be self-governing. Therefore, a state's attempt to regulate reservation Indians without congressional approval is inherently suspicious, the Supreme Court has said, given Congress's "overriding goal . . . of encouraging tribal self-sufficiency and economic development."[6]

Which state laws violate the federal preemption test?

Simply stated, a state law that is inconsistent with federal law violates the preemption test. Federal law is supreme, and it must be obeyed. For example, if a federal law prohibits states from taxing Indian land, a state tax on Indian land violates the preemption test.

State laws that disrupt an overall federal plan or policy will also violate the preemption test if the disruption is significant. The leading case on this point is *Warren Trading Post Co. v. Arizona Tax Commission*, decided by the Supreme Court in 1965. The issue in that case was whether Arizona could impose a "gross proceeds" tax (similar to an income tax) on a non-Indian-owned store that sold food and other items to Navajos on the Navajo reservation. The state tax did not expressly violate a federal law. However, virtually every aspect of Indian trade is regulated by the federal government. The state tax, the Court held, would disrupt this overall federal plan and was therefore preempted by federal law.

In similar fashion, the Supreme Court has ruled that a state cannot require Indians to pay income taxes on the money they earn from reservation employment, or require non-Indians who hunt on tribal land to comply with state hunting laws, because these state laws interfere with federal treaties and tribal laws.

The preemption test only goes so far, however, as illustrated by the Supreme Court's 1989 decision in *Cotton Petroleum Corp. v. New Mexico*. The issue in *Cotton Petroleum* was whether New Mexico could tax the oil and gas taken out of the ground ("produced") on tribal land by non-Indians. The tribe imposed its own tax on these producers. In challenging the state's tax, the tribe argued that it would be difficult to sell the tribe's oil and gas if producers had to pay two taxes instead of one. In addition, the tribe argued that the federal government already regulates oil and gas production on tribal land and the state's tax would disrupt the federal plan.

The Court upheld the state tax on a 6–3 vote. The Court admitted that the state tax could make the tribe's oil and gas less attractive to producers. However, there was no proof, the Court said, that the tribe would be unable to sell its oil and gas with the two taxes. The Court also said that, although there is some federal regulation of oil and gas on tribal land, it was not comprehensive enough to preempt New Mexico's tax.

Given *Cotton Petroleum*, it is clear that a limited amount of federal regulation is not enough to preempt a state law. What remains unclear is how much federal regulation is required. This clarity will come only after the Supreme Court decides additional cases on this subject.

Which state laws violate the infringement test?

In 1959 the Supreme Court held in *Williams v. Lee* that a state may not infringe "on the right of reservation Indians to make their own laws and be ruled by them."[7] This principle has become known as the infringement test. It protects the inherent right of Indian tribes to be self-governing.

In *Williams*, a non-Indian who owned a store on the Navajo reservation sued a member of the tribe in state court, seeking to collect a business debt. A tribal court was available to hear this case, but the store owner filed suit in state court anyway. The state court ruled in favor of the non-Indian. However, the U.S. Supreme Court reversed that decision. The Supreme Court held that the state court had no right to decide a case of this nature. The store owner had to use the tribal court because "to allow the exercise of state jurisdiction here would undermine the authority of the tribal courts over Reservation affairs and hence would infringe on the right of the Indians to govern themselves."[8]

The Supreme Court reached a similar conclusion in *Fisher v. District Court* (1976). The issue in *Fisher* was whether a state divorce court had the right to decide which parent would have custody of an Indian child. The child and both parents were reservation Indians. Applying the infringement test, the Court held that the state court had no right to hear this case. Allowing state court jurisdiction, the Court explained, would interfere with the powers of self-government because the tribe had already established a court to hear these cases.

Is the combination of the preemption and infringement tests equal in scope to the *Worcester* rule?

Not quite. The *Worcester* rule, created by the Supreme Court in 1832, prohibited *all* state laws from being enforced in Indian country if they didn't have congressional consent, even laws that applied only to non-Indians. The Supreme Court has modified this rule during the past 40 years and replaced it with the preemption and infringement tests. The combination of these tests is nearly as strong as the *Worcester* rule, especially with respect to state laws that affect Indians. Every effort by the states thus far to regulate an activity involving only reservation Indians has failed either the preemption or infringement test unless it was authorized by Congress. However, courts have allowed states to regulate some activities of non-Indians on the reservation, as *Cotton Petroleum* illustrates.

STATE JURISDICTION OVER OFF-RESERVATION INDIANS

What powers do the states have over off-reservation Indians?

When Indians are outside the reservation, even briefly, they are subject to the same state laws as everyone else unless a federal law or treaty grants an immunity. To illustrate, every state has laws limiting the seasons when hunting is allowed within the state. An Indian off the reservation must obey these laws unless he or she has a federal right to hunt out-of-season, as some Indians do.

8

CRIMINAL JURISDICTION IN INDIAN COUNTRY

What is "criminal jurisdiction"?

Every government has the right to make certain behavior illegal and to punish those who break laws. This is known as exercising criminal jurisdiction.

As a general rule, a government can exercise its criminal jurisdiction everywhere within its borders. Therefore, three governments can in theory apply their criminal laws on an Indian reservation: the tribe, the state in which the reservation is located, and the United States. However, Indian reservations are an exception to this general rule. On no Indian reservation can all three governments exercise their full criminal jurisdiction.

Criminal jurisdiction in Indian country is complicated. There are hundreds of laws and court decisions, issued randomly during the past 200 years, that together explain which government can arrest people in Indian country. However, four principles and three federal laws answer most questions on this subject.

What are the four principles governing criminal jurisdiction in Indian country?

1. An Indian tribe has the inherent right to exercise criminal jurisdiction over its members. As the Supreme Court has stated, "An Indian tribe's power to punish tribal offenders is part of its own retained sovereignty."[1]

2. Congress can reduce or eliminate all tribal powers, including a tribe's criminal jurisdiction. Therefore, although a tribe's criminal jurisdiction is inherent, it can be limited by Congress.

3. An Indian tribe lacks criminal jurisdiction over non-Indians unless Congress has expressly given it that power. The Supreme Court announced this principle in *Oliphant v. Suquamish Indian Tribe* in 1978. Thus, Indian tribes cannot arrest and imprison non-Indians without congressional authorization, and only a few tribes have clauses in their treaties authorizing criminal jurisdiction over non-Indians.

4. A state does not have criminal jurisdiction over Indians on the reservation, unless Congress has given it that power. Only a few states have been given the power to arrest reservation Indians.

These four principles may be summarized as follows: Congress has the ultimate authority to decide which government can exercise criminal jurisdiction in Indian country. Unless Congress has decided otherwise, a tribe can prosecute Indians but not non-Indians, and a state has no criminal jurisdiction over Indians in Indian country.

What are the three most important statutes regarding criminal jurisdiction in Indian country?

In 1832 in *Worcester v. Georgia*, the Supreme Court held that state criminal laws could not be applied in Indian country without the approval of Congress. Indian tribes, in other words, had exclusive criminal jurisdiction in Indian country until Congress decided otherwise.

Since then, Congress has passed several laws that changed criminal jurisdiction in Indian country. These laws allow the state or the federal government to exercise criminal jurisdiction in certain situations. The three most important laws are Public Law 83-280,[2] the General Crimes Act,[3] and the Major Crimes Act.[4] As a result of these laws, every Indian reservation is now subject to state or federal criminal jurisdiction to some extent.

Public Law 83-280: P.L. 280, as it is commonly known, was passed by Congress in 1953. This law required six states to exercise full criminal jurisdiction in Indian country. (These states are called the "mandatory" states.) The other 44 states were permitted to accept criminal jurisdiction at their option, and a few did. (They are called the "option" states.) The tables in chapter 7 list the states that acquired criminal jurisdiction under P.L. 280. Within these states, Indians are generally subject to the same criminal laws that apply to non-Indians and can be prosecuted in state court for crimes committed on the reservation.

On every reservation where state law does not govern Indian crimes, federal law applies. Congress has given the federal government certain criminal powers on all of these reservations by the General Crimes Act of 1834 (also known as the Indian Country Crimes Act) and the Major Crimes Act of 1885. But these laws do not give the federal government as much authority as P.L. 280 gives to the six mandatory states, which is full authority.

General Crimes Act: The General Crimes Act authorizes the federal government to extend all of its criminal laws into Indian country except for crimes committed by one Indian against the person or property of another Indian. Thus an Indian who robs a non-Indian on the reservation can be prosecuted by the federal government under the General Crimes Act, but if the same Indian robs another Indian, the act would not apply. In other words, the General Crimes Act did not change the rule that Indian tribes had exclusive jurisdiction over crimes committed by one reservation Indian against another.

Major Crimes Act: The Major Crimes Act was passed by Congress in response to *Ex parte Crow Dog*, a case decided by the Supreme Court in 1883. That case involved a Sioux Indian named Crow Dog who had been arrested by federal officers for murdering a Sioux chief, Spotted Tail, on a reservation in South Dakota. The Supreme Court ordered Crow Dog's release because, under the General Crimes Act, the government did not have jurisdiction over reservation crimes committed by one Indian against another. Congress was so upset by the *Crow Dog* decision that it passed the Major Crimes Act, which gave the federal government jurisdiction over seven major crimes when committed by an Indian against the person or property of any other person within Indian country. The Major Crimes Act has been amended several times and now covers more than a dozen crimes, including murder, rape, kidnapping, and assault with a deadly weapon. Thus, for these crimes, exclusive jurisdiction no longer rests with the tribe.

The tables below illustrate the pattern of criminal jurisdiction in Indian country in non–P.L. 280 states. The first table shows the pattern of jurisdiction when the crime committed is one of the crimes covered by the Major Crimes Act. The second table shows the jurisdictional pattern for all other crimes.

When the crime committed is a "major" crime

Persons Involved	Jurisdiction
Indian accused, Indian victim	Federal government (Major Crimes Act) and tribal government (inherent sovereignty)

Indian accused, non-Indian victim	Federal government (Major Crimes Act) and tribal government (inherent sovereignty)
Non-Indian accused, Indian victim	Federal government only (General Crimes Act)
Non-Indian accused, non-Indian victim	State government only

When the crime committed is not a "major" crime

Persons Involved	Jurisdiction
Indian accused, Indian victim	Tribal government only (inherent sovereignty)
Indian accused, non-Indian victim	Federal government (General Crimes Act) and tribal government (inherent sovereignty)
Non-Indian accused, Indian victim	Federal government only (General Crimes Act)
Non-Indian accused, non-Indian victim	State government only

Has the federal government been doing a good job in enforcing these criminal laws?

Generally, no. The federal government has been irresponsible in prosecuting serious crimes on many reservations. Studies show, for example, that violent crimes occur twice as often per capita on Indian reservations than elsewhere, with rape occurring four times as often. Yet the conviction rate is much lower than it is elsewhere. Of 802 reported felonies (crimes punishable by more than one year in prison) on the Navajo reservation during 1982 and 1983, there were only eighteen convictions, about 2 percent.[5] The problem exists in large part

93

because the federal government has not assigned sufficient law-enforcement resources and personnel to Indian reservations.[6] The FBI, which must investigate these federal crimes, has admitted that it gives reservation crime a low priority.[7] As a U.S. Justice Department report recently stated, "Law enforcement on Indian reservations is in serious trouble."[8]

CRIMES BY INDIANS AGAINST INDIANS IN NON-P.L. 280 STATES

What jurisdiction does the tribe have over a reservation crime committed by one Indian against another?

Indian tribes have the inherent right to enforce their criminal laws against tribal members. As stated earlier, this power is part of their retained sovereignty.

In 1990, the Supreme Court held that Indian tribes did not have the inherent right to exercise their criminal jurisdiction against non-member Indians (Indians who are not members of that tribe). In 1991, Congress responded to this ruling by passing a law authorizing tribes to exercise that power. Today, then, tribes have the right to prosecute all Indians, both members and non-members, who violate tribal law.

What jurisdiction does the state have over these crimes?

None, unless the state has been given this jurisdiction by Congress, as some states have. Without this authority, a state cannot prosecute Indians for crimes committed in Indian country.

As explained in the last chapter, state laws can apply in Indian country in some situations even without congressional consent. However, state jurisdiction is not permitted if it would seriously interfere with the ability of a tribe to govern itself.

State prosecution of reservation crimes by tribal members certainly would interfere with tribal self-government. "As a practical matter," the Supreme Court explained in 1979, "this has meant that criminal offenses by or against Indians have been subject only to federal or tribal laws, except where Congress . . . has expressly provided that State laws shall apply."[9]

Therefore, only those states authorized by Congress to prosecute reservation crimes by Indians can do so. These include the P.L. 280 states and a few others, as discussed later in this chapter.

What jurisdiction does the federal government have over these crimes?

The Major Crimes Act (MCA) gives the federal government criminal jurisdiction over more than a dozen major crimes committed by one reservation Indian against another. In addition to these major crimes, the federal government can also prosecute Indians who commit crimes that Congress intended to be crimes wherever they are committed, such as treason, counterfeiting, and assaulting a federal officer. (These are called "wherever committed" crimes.) For example, Congress has made it illegal for anyone to kill bald and golden eagles without a special license. In 1986, the Supreme Court held that a reservation Indian could be prosecuted for violating this law because Congress intended for this conduct to be a crime wherever it is committed.

If a tribe prosecutes an Indian, can the federal government later prosecute that person for the same offense?

The Fifth Amendment to the U.S. Constitution contains the Double Jeopardy Clause. This clause guarantees that no person shall be "subject for the same offense to be twice put in jeopardy of life or limb." The term "same offense" as used in the Double Jeopardy Clause applies to "lesser included" offenses. A lesser included offense is a crime necessarily committed whenever a greater offense occurs. For example, assault is always committed when a murder is committed; therefore, assault is a lesser included offense of murder. A person convicted of assault cannot be prosecuted for murder arising out of the same incident against the same victim. Similarly, a prosecution for murder precludes a later prosecution for assault, even if the person was found not guilty of murder.

The Supreme Court has held, however, that the Double Jeopardy Clause applies only to a second prosecution by the same government and not by different governments. In other words, if a person's conduct violates both state and federal law, both the state and federal government can prosecute that person.

In *United States v. Wheeler* in 1978, the Supreme Court had to decide whether the federal government could prosecute an Indian for statutory rape after a tribal court had convicted him of contributing to the delinquency of a minor, a lesser included offense. The defendant claimed that the Double Jeopardy Clause prevented a second prosecution. He argued that a tribal government is part of the federal government and, therefore, a second prosecution would constitute double jeopardy. The Supreme Court disagreed. In a decision of far-reaching significance, the Court recognized that Indian tribes are distinct and separate from the federal government, even though Congress may regulate them. Thus, the Double Jeopardy Clause did not prevent this second prosecution, and second conviction.

CRIMES BY INDIANS AGAINST NON-INDIANS IN NON-P.L. 280 STATES

Jurisdiction over crimes committed by Indians against non-Indians in Indian country follows the same pattern as the Indian-against-Indian crimes, with one significant difference. For reasons explained below, the federal government has greater jurisdiction over these offenses.

What jurisdiction does the tribe have over crimes committed by an Indian against a non-Indian in Indian country?

An Indian tribe has the inherent right to exercise its criminal jurisdiction against any Indian who violates tribal law, regardless of the race of the victim.

What jurisdiction does the state have over these crimes?

None, unless Congress has authorized the state to prosecute the Indians who commit them. Most states have not been given this authority. The tables in chapter 7 list the states that have such authority.

What jurisdiction does the federal government have over these crimes?

Congress has passed laws giving the federal government jurisdiction to prosecute every kind of crime committed by an Indian against a non-Indian in Indian country. (Given that the tribe can also prosecute these crimes, the tribe and the federal government have "concurrent" jurisdiction over them.) As previously explained, the General Crimes Act authorizes the federal government to prosecute any Indian who commits a crime against a non-Indian. In addition, the Major Crimes Act authorizes the federal government to prosecute an Indian who commits certain major crimes against anyone, Indian or non-Indian. The combined effect of these laws is to permit the government to prosecute Indians who commit any kind of crime against a non-Indian.

CRIMES BY NON-INDIANS AGAINST INDIANS IN NON-P.L. 280 STATES

As between the federal and tribal governments the jurisdictional pattern governing crimes by non-Indians against Indians in Indian country is simple: only the federal government has jurisdiction. The tribe has no jurisdiction over offenses committed by non-Indians, as explained earlier. The federal government, on the other hand, does have this authority. The General Crimes Act authorizes the federal government to prosecute non-Indians who violate any of the government's criminal laws against an Indian.

As for state jurisdiction, the situation is unclear. Several courts have held that the General Crimes Act eliminates the state's power to prosecute non-Indians for crimes against Indians in Indian country. Most states do not prosecute these crimes. However, the act itself says nothing about this subject, and therefore it can be argued that the state can prosecute these non-Indians. (As explained earlier, this would not be considered double jeopardy, but Congress could still have removed the state's authority to prosecute these crimes when it passed the General Crimes Act.) To remove the uncertainty, it would be helpful if Congress would amend the General Crimes Act and declare one way or the other whether states can exercise criminal jurisdiction over these crimes.

CRIMES BY NON-INDIANS AGAINST NON-INDIANS

In the 1832 case of *Worcester v. Georgia,* the Supreme Court held that a state has no criminal jurisdiction in Indian country without congressional consent, even over crimes committed by non-Indians. The Court later changed this decision, however. (Every court can reverse itself, although this does not happen often.) In *United States v. McBratney* in 1881, the Court held that a state could prosecute a non-Indian who murdered another non-Indian in Indian country. It is now accepted that states can prosecute non-Indians for crimes against other non-Indians in Indian country.

The tribe has no jurisdiction over these crimes. As explained earlier, the Supreme Court held in 1978 that Indian tribes lack criminal jurisdiction over non-Indians.

The federal government does not have jurisdiction, either, unless the crime is a federal crime wherever committed, such as assaulting a federal officer. Thus the state has exclusive jurisdiction over these crimes. This means that unless the state exercises its jurisdiction, non-Indians who commit crimes against other non-Indians on the reservation will not be prosecuted. Unfortunately, on some reservations, state law-enforcement officers have been reluctant to investigate and prosecute these crimes because they do not want to spend their time and money solving them. To help relieve this problem, some states have given tribal police officers the authority to arrest non-Indians for violations of state law ("cross-deputizing"). When an arrest is made, the tribal officer then delivers the person into the custody of state officials for prosecution in state court.

CRIMINAL JURISDICTION IN P.L. 280 STATES

It has long been the rule that state criminal laws do not apply in Indian country unless Congress has authorized the state to enforce them there. The one exception to this rule (the *McBratney* exception) is that a state can prosecute offenses committed by one non-Indian against another non-Indian. Until fairly recently, this was the extent of the state's jurisdiction. However, in 1953 Congress enacted Public Law 280, which changed this situation.

What is the effect of P.L. 280?

Chapter 7 discusses Public Law 280. Essentially, this law requires six "mandatory" states to enforce their criminal laws in Indian country to the same extent that they enforce them elsewhere within the state. These six states are Alaska, California, Minnesota, Nebraska, Oregon, and Wisconsin. In addition, a few of the remaining "option" states accepted some amount of criminal jurisdiction in Indian country.

The tables in chapter 7 illustrate the extent to which the mandatory and option states have criminal jurisdiction in Indian country today. To the extent that they do, reservation Indians in those states can be arrested by state police officers and tried in state courts like other citizens of the state.

Several option states assumed partial, and not complete, criminal jurisdiction in Indian country. Therefore, in these states, the state will prosecute some crimes and the federal government will prosecute others (under the federal laws discussed earlier).

Are there any limits to the state's criminal jurisdiction under P.L. 280?

Yes. Public Law 280 contains a "savings" clause, which expressly removes certain things from state jurisdiction. The most important of these exemptions concerns Indian hunting and fishing rights, and use of land owned by the federal government (trust land). P.L. 280 provides that the states—even the mandatory states—cannot make it illegal for Indians to exercise their federal rights to hunt, fish, and use federal land. Thus, even P.L. 280 states cannot apply all of their criminal laws in Indian country.

Did P.L. 280 abolish the tribe's criminal jurisdiction?

Probably not, although the Supreme Court has yet to resolve this issue. The courts that have considered this question have held that P.L. 280 did not limit the tribe's criminal jurisdiction. Tribes located in P.L. 280 states have the right to prosecute tribal members under tribal law, and the state may prosecute them under state law, even for the same offense. As stated earlier, it does not violate the Double Jeopardy Clause when two different governments punish someone for the same crime.

Have any other states received criminal jurisdiction in Indian country besides the P.L. 280 states?

Yes, at least five states have. Specific acts of Congress have given Iowa, Kansas, Maine, New York, and Oklahoma some criminal jurisdiction in Indian country, somewhat similar to the powers received under P.L. 280.

PROBLEMS RELATING TO EXTRADITION

It often happens that a person will commit a crime in one state and flee to another state to escape prosecution. Extradition provides the means by which the "victim" state (the state where the crime was committed) can arrest and obtain custody of this person from the "asylum" state (the state to which the person fled). The U.S. Constitution provides that if one state is asked by the governor of another state to "deliver up" a person accused of a crime, it must comply with that request.[10] This constitutional provision is known as the Extradition Clause.

Tribal governments can become involved with extradition procedures in three situations: when an Indian commits a crime on the reservation and flees elsewhere; when an Indian commits a crime off the reservation and flees to the reservation; and when a non-Indian commits a crime off the reservation and flees to the reservation. Indian tribes, then, sometimes seek extradition and sometimes are asked to extradite.

Does the Extradition Clause apply to tribal governments?

Probably not. A century ago the Supreme Court held that no portion of the Constitution applies to the operation of tribal government unless Congress has expressly made it applicable. Congress has not made the Extradition Clause applicable to Indian tribes; accordingly, courts have held that it is inapplicable. This specific issue has yet to reach the Supreme Court. As it now stands, tribes need not return a person who has fled to the reservation, and a state need not return an Indian who has fled from the reservation. The constitutional provision regarding extradition applies only when two states are involved.

In order to avoid the appearance of harboring criminals and to assist each other in prosecuting lawbreakers, many tribes and their surrounding states have entered into extradition agreements. This type of mutual effort should be encouraged.

Are state officers allowed to enter the reservation and arrest a non-Indian who has committed a crime in state territory?

Probably. Under the *McBratney* rule, the state has jurisdiction over crimes committed by non-Indians against other non-

Indians within the reservation. Given that the state can enter the reservation to arrest these offenders, it can probably also enter the reservation to arrest non-Indians who have committed crimes off the reservation.

Most courts have held, though, that state officials do not have the right to enter the reservation and arrest a tribal member who has committed a crime off the reservation. The Supreme Court has not yet addressed either of these questions of state jurisdiction.

Which government has jurisdiction over off-reservation crimes committed by Indians?

The state. An Indian who engages in an activity outside the reservation that is a crime under state law can be punished in the same fashion as a non-Indian who commits that crime. The only exception to this rule occurs when an Indian has an immunity under federal law. For example, Indians who have a federal-treaty right to fish off their reservation do not have to comply with state law in exercising that right.

9

CIVIL JURISDICTION IN INDIAN COUNTRY

What is "civil jurisdiction"?

Every government has two broad powers: criminal jurisdiction and civil jurisdiction. Criminal jurisdiction maintains law and order. Civil jurisdiction maintains everything else, particularly a society's culture and values. Most family matters, such as marriage, divorce, child custody, and adoptions, and most property matters, such as the sale of goods and services, taxation, land use, and inheritance, are regulated through the government's civil jurisdiction. Thus, exercising civil jurisdiction is vitally important for every government.

TRIBAL JURISDICTION

**Does an Indian tribe have the right to exercise
civil jurisdiction?**

Yes. An Indian tribe has the inherent right to exercise civil jurisdiction within the territory it controls.[1] This right is as important to an Indian tribe as it is to every other government.

No one questions the fact that an Indian tribe may exercise the full range of its civil jurisdiction over tribal members within the reservation. Tribal members, for example, who wish to marry, divorce, adopt children, develop their land, or engage in business on the reservation can do so only if they comply with tribal law.

With regard to non-Indians, the rule is almost the same, but there are a few exceptions to the tribe's jurisdiction. As explained in the last chapter, the Supreme Court held in 1978 that an Indian tribe lacks criminal jurisdiction over non-Indians unless Congress has given it that power. Regarding civil jurisdiction, the rule is just the opposite, at least with respect to activities of non-Indians that significantly affect the tribe's economy, health, welfare, or ability to be self-governing. As the Supreme Court stated in 1980, Indian tribes may exercise "a broad range of civil jurisdiction over the activities of non-Indians on Indian reservation lands in which the tribes have a significant interest."[2] In other words, Congress does not have to authorize a tribe's civil jurisdiction over non-Indians; this power is presumed to exist. Civil jurisdiction over Indians and non-Indians is an important part of tribal sovereignty.

Courts have upheld tribal civil jurisdiction over non-Indians in a wide range of situations. For the most part, non-Indians who enter the reservation become fully subject to the tribe's civil powers. Tribes can tax the personal property, such as a car, mobile home, or cattle, owned by non-Indians on the reservation. Tribes can also tax non-Indian companies doing business on the reservation. Non-Indians who sell things on the reservation must get a tribal license and comply with tribal law, and can be charged a tribal sales tax when they buy things on the reservation. A tribe can regulate hunting and fishing by non-Indians on tribal land. A tribe also can enforce its clean air and water regulations on non-Indians within the reservation. Even tribes located in the "mandatory" Public Law 83-280 states (discussed in chapter 7) retain this inherent power; nothing in P.L. 280 takes this right away from tribes.

A tribe lacks jurisdiction only when the non-Indian's conduct does not significantly affect tribal interests. For example, when two non-Indians on the reservation want to get a divorce, they must comply with state law and not tribal law, because the tribe does not have a sufficient interest to impose its laws on them. However, if one spouse is a tribal member, the tribe's interest in regulating tribal members and their property is enough to make the divorce subject to tribal law. The same is true for a car accident on the reservation: if one person involved in the accident is a tribal member, any lawsuit involving that member must be brought in tribal court rather than state court. In short, virtually every activity by a non-Indian on the reservation that involves Indians or Indian property is subject to the tribe's civil jurisdiction.

Can non-Indians be sued in tribal court?

Yes, with respect to activities that involve an Indian or the tribe. Tribal courts, as with state and federal courts, help enforce the government's civil jurisdiction. On most reservations, the tribal court is authorized either by the tribe's constitution or by a tribal law to resolve disputes concerning Indians, even when non-Indians are involved. Therefore, non-Indians can sue, and be sued, in tribal court for activities that take place on the reservation involving Indians or the tribe. In the above example involving the car accident, the Indian and non-Indian could sue each other in tribal court to determine which driver was at fault.

Can a non-Indian who is sued in tribal court challenge the court's jurisdiction?

Yes. As just explained, a tribe cannot exercise its civil jurisdiction over non-Indians when (1) Congress has removed the tribe's power, or (2) the tribe lacks a sufficient interest in regulating the activity in question. Non-Indians sued in tribal court can argue that one of these exceptions to the tribe's jurisdiction is present. In *National Farmers Union Insurance Co. v. Crow Tribe of Indians* (1985), the Supreme Court held that the question of whether a tribe has jurisdiction in a particular case is a "federal question," and therefore federal courts have the final say. In other words, a federal court can decide that an Indian tribe does not have jurisdiction over a non-Indian in a particular situation.

However, *National Farmers Union* also held that non-Indians who challenge the tribe's jurisdiction must first raise the issue in tribal court before raising it in federal court. "Congress is committed to a policy of supporting tribal self-government and self-determination," the Supreme Court noted, and imposing this "exhaustion requirement" is consistent with this federal policy.[3]

Non-Indians do not have to exhaust tribal remedies if the tribe does not have a court system or if it would be unreasonably slow. However, this is rarely the case. Thus, non-Indians who enter the reservation and become involved with Indians or their property should assume that they are subject to the tribe's civil jurisdiction, and that they may have to defend their conduct in a tribal court.

STATE JURISDICTION

Does the state have the right to exercise civil jurisdiction in Indian country?

Immediately after the United States became a nation, state governments tried to extend their laws into Indian territory in a deliberate effort to change Indian culture and control Indian life. The Supreme Court, however, declared almost every one of these attempts to be illegal. But the Supreme Court has not always been a friend to the Indians. At times, the Court has been an enemy, as some of the Court's recent decisions illustrate. However, tribes would have little civil jurisdiction today —and the states would have much more control over Indians than they do—if the Supreme Court had not protected the rights of tribes so vigorously.

As early as 1832, in *Worcester v. Georgia*, the Supreme Court established the rule that state officials can exercise only that authority within Indian country that Congress has *expressly* given them. Without express congressional approval, states cannot interfere with the inherent right of tribes to regulate their internal affairs.

Today, civil jurisdiction in Indian country remains almost entirely a tribal matter. This is because (1) Congress has rarely authorized states to extend their laws into Indian country, and (2) the Supreme Court has defended the right of Indian tribes to remain free of state control unless Congress has given that consent.

However, the Supreme Court has somewhat relaxed the *Worcester* rule, and state governments may now extend certain laws into Indian country without Congress's consent. As explained in chapter 7, the Supreme Court has replaced the *Worcester* rule with two tests: the infringement test and the federal preemption test. If a state law passes these two tests, it can be enforced in Indian country even though Congress has not given its approval.

The infringement and federal preemption tests are very difficult tests to pass. In practice, they create a barrier nearly as formidable as the *Worcester* rule. The Supreme Court has decided many cases in which it has used these two tests, and in almost every case, the state was prevented from exercising its civil powers in Indian country.

Many of these cases involved taxation. States are constantly trying to think of ways to tax Indians and tribes—and non-Indians doing business with them—without the consent of Congress. The following state taxes, unauthorized by Congress, were invalidated by the Supreme Court: a tax on (1) the income earned by Indians who live and work on the reservation; (2) the personal property owned by Indians on the reservation; (3) the sale of goods by Indians to other Indians on the reservation; (4) the sale of goods by non-Indians to Indians on the reservation; (5) the profits made by an off-reservation non-Indian company that sold farm equipment to an Indian tribe; (6) the profits made by a non-Indian company that built a school for a tribe on its reservation; and (7) the income a tribe received when it leased tribal land for mineral development. (Thus, as discussed in the next chapter, reservation Indians pay almost no state taxes.)

States have also attempted to enforce many other kinds of laws in Indian country without the consent of Congress. Almost all of these efforts have failed. For example, courts have held that, without express authority from Congress, (1) state courts may not decide divorce cases involving reservation Indians, even if one spouse is non-Indian; (2) state courts may not resolve reservation contract disputes between Indians and non-Indians; (3) state courts may not decide adoption cases involving reservation Indian children and their parents; (4) states cannot require non-Indians who hunt on tribal land to purchase a state hunting license; and (5) a state has no authority to regulate billboards, hazardous waste, or the rental of Indian property on the reservation. As these cases illustrate, state officials generally may not extend state laws into Indian country, and state courts may not resolve disputes arising within Indian country, when Indians are involved (even if non-Indians are also involved).

In a number of these court cases, such as those involving business activities on the reservation, the state was able to show that it had an interest in regulating the tribe's activity because it affected the state. However, in all of these cases, the state's interest was secondary to the tribe's interest in self-government. A state is only allowed to protect its interest, the Supreme Court has held, "up to the point where tribal self-government would be affected," unless Congress has expressly authorized the state to act.[4] The same rule applies between two states. For example, when Nevada allowed gambling in Las Vegas, this hurt some businesses in California, but this did not mean that California could then regulate what was going on in Nevada. Likewise, just because a tribal activity affects a state does not mean that the state has a right to regulate it.

The Supreme Court, however, has allowed states to regulate certain activities of *non*-Indians on the reservation, even when this creates some burdens for the tribe. For example, the Court has held that a tribal business can be required by the state to collect a state sales tax on the goods it sells to non-Indians, even though these taxes make the tribe's goods more expensive. States can also tax the personal property a non-Indian owns on the reservation, even if the tribe taxes the same property. The same is true for oil and gas produced on the reservation by a non-Indian company: the state can tax it even though these producers are already paying a tribal tax. This subject is discussed in more detail in the next chapter.

What civil jurisdiction has Congress expressly authorized the states to have in Indian country?

Only rarely has Congress authorized a state to extend its civil powers into Indian country. These few powers are discussed in chapter 7. Many states have asked Congress to increase their powers in Indian country, but Congress has preferred to leave civil jurisdiction primarily in tribal hands.

May a state "serve process" on an Indian within the reservation for something that occurred off the reservation?

As chapter 7 explains, Indians who leave the reservation are subject to state jurisdiction unless they are engaging in an activity that is protected by federal law. A reservation Indian, therefore, who causes an automobile accident while off the reservation can be sued for damages in state court.

No lawsuit can begin until the plaintiff files with the court a summons and complaint, and the defendant is personally served with a copy of them. This is called "service of process."

Most courts in considering this question have held that Indians may be served with process on the reservation for their off-reservation activities. The Supreme Court has not answered this question directly, but in a recent case it permitted a state lawsuit to proceed where the Indians who were being sued had been served with process on the reservation. The Court apparently saw nothing wrong with this procedure.

May a state court enforce a judgment against an Indian by seizing reservation property owned by that person?

When a person is sued for money and loses the case, the court issues a "judgment" ordering that person (the "judgment debtor") to pay the amount of money awarded by the court. If the money is not paid, the court can order court officials to seize and sell property belonging to the debtor so that the judgment can be paid.

As a general rule, a court may not seize property located outside its geographic jurisdiction. Accordingly, a state court cannot seize Indian property located on a reservation because this territory is beyond the court's jurisdiction. The procedure that should be followed to collect the money owed in this situation is described below.

Must state and tribal governments give "full faith and credit" to each other's laws and court decrees?

The U.S. Constitution expressly requires each state to give "full faith and credit" to the laws and court decisions of another state.[5] Thus if you get married in Florida and later move to New York, you do not have to get married again. Likewise, if you have a driver's license issued from one state, you can legally drive through any other state. If states were free to ignore the laws and decrees of sister states, there would be chaos, which is why the Constitution contains the Full Faith and Credit Clause.

There is nothing in the Constitution that requires a state and a tribe to give full faith and credit to each other's laws and court decisions. However, to avoid a similar chaos, some courts have held that states and tribes must extend full faith and credit to one another. Several states and tribes have passed laws that require that they do so.

Therefore, a non-Indian who obtains a judgment in state court against an Indian, as in the situation mentioned earlier, should be able to enforce it through the tribal court. The non-Indian would show the state court judgment to the tribal court, and that court would order tribal officials to seize and sell the Indian's reservation property to pay off the debt.

If states and tribes do not extend full faith and credit to one another, this can cause serious problems for Indians and non-Indians. For instance, reservation Indians will have difficulty purchasing goods on credit, or borrowing money, outside the reservation if businesses and lenders are unable to enforce state court decisions in tribal court. It is in everyone's best interest for tribes and states to extend full faith and credit to each other's laws and court decrees. Federal courts, as well, should give full faith and credit to tribal laws and court decisions.

FEDERAL JURISDICTION

Which civil laws have the federal government been authorized to apply in Indian country?

Federal civil laws, like state civil laws, cannot be applied in Indian county without the approval of Congress. Congress has given such authorization in a few specific areas. As explained in chapter 5, federal officials have authority to regulate reservation trade with Indians; control the sale, use, and inheritance of Indian trust land; and control the sale and use of natural resources, such as timber, oil, gas, and other minerals. The tribe is permitted to regulate in these areas as well, provided that its laws do not conflict with federal laws.

Apart from these areas, Congress has allowed Indian tribes to remain relatively free from the federal government's civil powers. The same is true for the state's civil jurisdiction, as explained earlier. As a consequence, civil jurisdiction on the reservation is almost entirely tribal.

10

TAXATION

Taxes are the lifeblood of government. Governments need money for construction projects (such as roads and schools), to pay their employees, and to run government programs. The primary means of raising this money is taxation. If you live or work on an Indian reservation, or do business there, you may find yourself being taxed by three governments: tribal, state, and federal. Below is an explanation of which taxes you should expect to pay.

Three terms are used in this chapter that need to be defined: "trust," "deeded" land, and "allotted" land. *Trust* land is owned by the federal government. However, it has been set aside for the use of an Indian or tribe. The Indian or tribe assigned this land is called the beneficial owner (as opposed to the true owner, which is the federal government).

In addition to having trust land, Indians and tribes can own land themselves. This privately owned land is called *deeded* land because a deed of ownership has been issued to it. Indians and tribes can obtain deeded land by purchasing

114

it, inheriting it, or being given it, just as everyone else can.

Beginning with the General Allotment Act of 1887, the federal government began taking trust land assigned to a tribe and giving portions of it to tribal members: 160 acres to every head of household, and 80 acres to every unmarried adult. (Why Congress did this, and the disaster it caused, is discussed in chapters 1 and 5.) These portions of land—called *allotted* land or allotments—were then held in trust by the federal government for that person. Years later, the federal government started giving some Indians a deed to their allotment. Once the deed was given, the Indian owned the land and could sell it, and many of these allotments were sold to non-Indians. Today, then, many allotments are privately owned (deeded land) while others are still owned by the federal government (trust land).

In 1934 Congress ended the practice of taking land from tribes against their will and allotting it to tribal members. However, thousands of trust allotments had already been issued, and special tax rules apply to this land.

FEDERAL TAXATION

Must Indians pay federal income taxes?

Yes. In *Squire v. Capoeman* (1956), the Supreme Court held that Indians must pay federal income taxes unless a treaty or statute gives them an exemption. The Court said: "We agree with the Government that Indians are citizens and that in ordinary affairs of life, not governed by treaty or remedial legislation, they are subject to the payment of income taxes as are other citizens."[1]

In most other areas of federal Indian law, the rule is just the reverse. Usually, a federal law does not apply to reservation Indians unless Congress expressly says it does. A federal tax law, in contrast, applies to reservation Indians unless Congress expressly says it does not. Indians, whether on the reservation or off, generally must pay the same federal taxes as everyone else. These would include federal income taxes, Social Security taxes, and federal taxes on gasoline, alcohol, and cigarettes.

Has Congress given Indians any exemptions from federal taxation?

Only three. First, Congress has passed a law that exempts from taxation any money paid by the federal government as compensation for the taking of property. The Just Compensation Clause of the Fifth Amendment to the Constitution requires the federal government to pay fair compensation whenever it takes away someone's private property. (For example, if you owned some land and the government took it to build an airport, the government must pay you the fair market value of the land.) During the 1800s, many tribes signed treaties in which they obtained reservations of land in the West. As the population of the United States grew and spread westward, the federal government began taking much of this land from the tribes. The Supreme Court has held that these tribes are entitled to recover fair compensation for the land, including the value of any minerals, water rights, hunting and fishing rights, and other interests found on or in the land. A federal law exempts this type of income from federal taxation.

Second, Congress has passed a law (part of the General Allotment Act) that exempts from federal taxation all income earned directly from an Indian's trust allotment. Indians, for example, who farm or ranch on their trust land, or sell timber or minerals from it, do not have to pay federal income taxes on the money they earn. Third, Indians do not have to pay inheritance (estate) taxes when they inherit a trust allotment.

116

As just mentioned, Indians have a tax exemption under the General Allotment Act, but this exemption has been given a narrow interpretation by the courts, in two respects. First, the courts have held that the act exempts only the income an Indian earns from his or her *own* trust allotment. If an Indian earns money from someone else's allotment, that income is taxable. To illustrate, if an Indian owns two oil wells, one on her allotment and one on an allotment she leases from another Indian, the income made from the leased land is taxable.

Second, the immunity does not cover "reinvestment" income. If an Indian takes the money she earns from her trust allotment (which is not taxable) and then reinvests it, the money earned is taxable. In the illustration above, if the Indian took the money she earned from the oil well on her allotment and put it into a bank account, the interest she earned on the account is taxable.

To summarize, Indians normally must pay the same federal taxes everyone else pays, including federal income taxes. However, Indians are not taxed on their compensation funds, they are not taxed on income earned from their own trust allotments, and they are not taxed on the value of a trust allotment they inherit.

To what extent are Indian tribes taxed by the federal government?

Congress has passed laws that give the state governments an immunity from most federal taxes. These laws do not mention Indian tribes. In 1982 a federal court ruled that Indian tribes were not exempt from federal taxation because no immunity had been expressly conferred by Congress.

In response to this court decision, Congress passed the Indian Tribal Governmental Tax Status Act of 1988. This law provides Indian tribes with the same basic exemptions from federal taxation that the states enjoy. For instance, tribes (and states) do not pay taxes on any income they earn from businesses they own.

STATE TAXATION

Chapter 7 explains that a state is, in general, not permitted to enforce its laws on an Indian reservation without congressional approval. The Constitution gives Congress supreme authority to regulate tribal affairs. A state law that interferes with this supreme power is "preempted" by federal law. This "preemption" doctrine draws support from the fact that an Indian tribe has the inherent right to be self-governing and to regulate its own internal matters unless limited by Congress.

This rule applies to state tax laws. The Supreme Court has decided at least ten cases involving an attempt by a state to tax reservation Indians or tribes without Congress's approval. In every case but one, the Court invalidated the tax. (The one exception, discussed below, involved a state tax on a tribe's sales to *non*-Indians.) As the Supreme Court noted in 1985, "Indian tribes and individuals generally are exempt from state taxation within their own territory."[2]

State Taxation of Reservation Indians

Do reservation Indians have to pay state income taxes?

No. The Supreme Court ruled in 1973 that Indians who live on the reservation do not have to pay state income taxes on money they earn on the reservation.

Do reservation Indians have to pay state personal property taxes?

No. In 1976 the Supreme Court held that personal property (such

as cars and mobile homes) on the reservation owned by a tribal
member is exempt from state taxation. Similarly, a state may not
tax the personal property of an Indian-owned business within the
reservation. If an Indian marries a non-Indian, the personal property they own on the reservation is not taxable by the state even
though half of it may be said to belong to the non-Indian spouse.
(Only if the property is owned entirely by the non-Indian spouse
could the state tax it. For example, if the non-Indian owned a car
that was registered only to him or her, the state could tax it.)

Do reservation Indians have to pay a state sales tax on purchases made within the reservation?

No. Indians who purchase goods or services on their reservation cannot be charged a state sales tax, the Supreme Court has
held. This is true whether the seller is an Indian, a non-Indian,
or a tribe, and even if the item is to be used off the reservation.

Can a state impose a real estate tax on Indian or tribal trust land?

No. As explained earlier, trust land is owned by the federal government and set aside for the use of an Indian or tribe. A state
may not tax federal land; therefore, all trust land is immune
from state taxation.

Permanent attachments to land, such as a house, a fence,
or a well, are considered to be part of the land. Therefore, the
value of these improvements cannot be taxed when they are
attached to trust land.

What other state taxes have been invalidated, and which ones do Indians have to pay?

Only rarely has Congress authorized state taxation of reservation Indians. Consequently, there are few state taxes that they
must pay.

Occasionally, a law passed by Congress is unclear as to whether it is authorizing state taxation on the reservation. The Supreme Court has established the rule that Indians and tribes remain free from a state tax unless an approval from Congress to impose it is "unmistakably clear."[3] Using this rule, the Supreme Court has invalidated several state taxes. For example, a law passed by Congress in 1940 authorizes states to impose income and sales taxes in any "Federal area," such as on military bases. In 1965 the Supreme Court held that this general law does not authorize state taxation on Indian reservations because Congress did not give its clear permission to have it applied there.

Congress has passed a few laws that consent to state taxation of reservation Indians and tribes, but only a few. One law authorizes states to tax sales of liquor to Indians. Another law, part of the General Allotment Act, authorizes the state to assess real estate taxes on allotments of Indian land after a deed is issued and the land becomes privately owned. (Given that deeds have been issued on millions of acres of Indian land, this law has given states considerable taxing power.)

Is the state allowed to tax Indians when they are outside the reservation?

When Indians are off the reservation, they are fully subject to state taxation unless a federal treaty or law confers an immunity. Few such immunities exist. Thus, as a general rule, Indians must pay (1) state sales taxes whenever they purchase something off the reservation, (2) state income taxes on income earned off the reservation, and (3) state real estate taxes on deeded land outside the reservation. Likewise, if an Indian or tribe operates a business outside the reservation, its income can be taxed by the state.

Can a state refuse to provide services to reservation Indians on the grounds that they are exempt from state taxation?

No. Indians may not be denied the full rights of state citizenship even though they are exempt from most state taxes. For example, Indians cannot be denied the right to vote in state elections simply because they do not pay real estate taxes on their trust allotments of land.

Indians have long enjoyed an immunity from most state taxes because of federal laws and treaties protecting them and their property. This protection was given to the Indians in exchange for their relinquishing vast amounts of land to the federal and state governments.

Non-Indians frequently claim that a state loses a lot of money by having an Indian reservation within its borders. This argument ignores the fact that Indians have already "paid" for their tax immunities by having exchanged land for them. Moreover, in most cases this argument is not accurate. First of all, most states spend a relatively small amount of money to provide services to Indians, because the federal government reimburses the state for the majority of the expense. Second, Indians eventually spend most of the money they earn from reservation employment, or receive from grants and programs, outside the reservation. These off-reservation sales are taxed by the state. The state also taxes the income received by the stores where these sales are made. Thus, few states suffer financially, and many prosper, because an Indian reservation is located within their borders.

Are nonmember Indians entitled to these same tax immunities?

Indians who are on a different reservation than their own (nonmember Indians) are not entitled to the same tax immunities enjoyed by members of that tribe. For example, although tribal members are exempt from paying state sales taxes on goods purchased on the reservation, the Supreme Court held in 1980 that nonmember Indians do not share that immunity.

State Taxation of Indian Tribes

A state may not tax an Indian tribe unless Congress has given its express consent. The Supreme Court has held, for instance, that states may not tax the money a tribe receives when the tribe sells its oil to non-Indians because Congress has not approved that tax.

There are two exceptions to this rule. First, states can tax tribal businesses located *off* the reservation, unless Congress has given the tribe an immunity. (As explained in the next chapter, some tribal fishing businesses have been given this immunity.)

Second, states can impose certain "collect and pass on" taxes. These are taxes that are paid by a non-Indian, which are collected by the tribe and then given to the state. To illustrate, the Supreme Court has held that a state can require a tribe to collect the state's sales tax when the tribe sells cigarettes to a non-Indian. However, in that case, the Court noted that the cigarettes were not manufactured by the tribe nor made with tribal products. In contrast, courts have invalidated "collect and pass on" laws that taxed sales of tribal timber and minerals to non-Indians because the state was providing nothing in return for the money it was getting from taxing the sale of these tribal resources.

In holding that tribes are required to collect and pass on state taxes when they sell certain items to non-Indians, the

Supreme Court admitted that this imposed a burden on tribes, but the Court characterized it as being "minimal."[4] The Court also admitted that allowing the state to tax these sales could hurt tribal businesses. After all, if a tribe did not have to charge a state sales tax when it sold items like cigarettes, its prices would be lower than off-reservation businesses, and this would attract customers. The Court held, however, that tribes are not entitled to such an "artificial" advantage.[5] Therefore, states can require tribes to collect sales taxes on their sales to non-Indians in these situations.

In short, Indian tribes cannot be taxed by state governments except with respect to off-reservation activities, and certain sales to non-Indians. Apart from that, Indian tribes remain free from state taxation because Congress has not consented to it.

State Taxation of Reservation Non-Indians

Do non-Indians on the reservation have to pay state taxes?

Most taxes, yes. As explained in chapter 7, a state law may not be enforced within Indian country if its enforcement would (1) violate a federal law or treaty (the preemption test), or (2) infringe on the right of the tribe to make its own laws and be ruled by them (the infringement test).

Most state taxes, when imposed on reservation non-Indians, will pass these tests. Of course, the enforcement of any state law on the reservation infringes to some extent on tribal self-government. The Supreme Court has held, however, that minimal infringements are permitted. Taxes that apply exclusively to non-Indians are allowed. State income taxes, personal property taxes, real estate taxes, gasoline taxes, and cigarette taxes have all been upheld by the courts when imposed on reservation non-Indians and their property.

However, just because the taxpayer is a non-Indian does not necessarily mean that a tax is valid. What matters most is where the tax *burden* falls. If the burden falls on an Indian or tribe, the tax is probably invalid. For example, a non-Indian company that builds a school for an Indian tribe will charge the tribe a higher price if state taxes must be paid. Therefore, the burden of that tax would fall on the tribe. In a 1980 case involving those facts, the Supreme Court invalidated the state tax, even though it was assessed on a non-Indian business. Similarly, in a 1965 case, the Court held that a state cannot tax non-Indian merchants on their reservation sales to Indians because, although non-Indians pay the tax, the tax burden falls on the Indian customers, who will have to pay a higher price for the merchant's goods.

In summary, although the infringement and federal preemption tests protect Indians and tribes from most state taxes, they offer limited protection to reservation non-Indians. This is because state taxation of non-Indians rarely interferes substantially with tribal government (the infringement test) or violates federal law (the preemption test). In fact, as explained below, non-Indians on the reservation not only have to pay most state taxes but also most tribal taxes.

TRIBAL TAXATION

May an Indian tribe tax its members?

Yes. An Indian tribe has the inherent right, as part of its sovereign powers, to tax its members. A tribe may impose the same taxes on its citizens as the federal and state governments impose on theirs.

May an Indian tribe tax nonmembers, including non-Indians, on the reservation?

Yes. Indian tribes have vast taxing powers, similar to the state and federal governments. As early as 1904 the Supreme Court held that an Indian tribe can tax personal property owned by a non-Indian on the reservation. In 1982 in *Merrion v. Jicarilla Apache Tribe*, the Supreme Court confirmed the inherent right of tribal taxation over all persons on the reservation. The Court stated:

> *The power to tax is an essential attribute of Indian sovereignty because it is a necessary instrument of self-government and territorial management. This power enables a tribal government to raise revenues for its essential services. . . . [The power to tax] derives from the tribe's general authority, as sovereign, to control economic activity within its jurisdiction, and to defray the cost of providing governmental services by requiring contributions from persons or enterprises engaged in economic activities within that jurisdiction.*[6]

In *Merrion*, the Court held that an Indian tribe could tax a non-Indian oil company on the value of oil it was extracting from tribal land.

Thus, non-Indians on the reservation can be taxed by the tribe. Courts have upheld a wide variety of such taxes, including sales, business, and personal property taxes.

Non-Indians sometimes argue that tribal taxes constitute "taxation without representation" because they cannot vote in tribal elections. But the fact is, the federal and state governments also tax people who cannot vote in their elections. Aliens (citizens of other countries who are living in the U.S.) cannot vote in federal or state elections, but they must pay federal and state income taxes. Likewise, residents of New

York who buy something in Connecticut will pay a Connecticut sales tax but cannot vote in Connecticut's elections. The fact that non-Indians cannot become members of a tribe or vote in tribal elections does not deprive the tribe of the right to tax them.

11

HUNTING, FISHING, AND GATHERING RIGHTS

Hunting, fishing, and gathering have always been important to Indians. Most tribes obtained all of their food this way. Access to wildlife, the Supreme Court has noted, was "not much less necessary to the existence of the Indians than the atmosphere they breathed."[1] Many tribes followed migrations of deer, elk, bison, and anadromous fish such as salmon and trout. (Anadromous fish are born in freshwater, migrate to the ocean, where they reach maturity, and complete their life cycle by returning on one or more occasions to the place where they were born to spawn.) The extent to which fishing was vital to the tribes in the state of Washington was explained by the Supreme Court in 1979:

> One hundred and twenty-five years ago . . . anadromous fish were even more important to most of the population of western Washington than they are today. At that time, about three-fourths of the approximately 10,000 inhabitants of the area were Indians.

*Although in some respects the cultures of the different
tribes varied . . . all of them shared a vital and unifying dependence on anadromous fish.*

*Religious rites were intended to insure the continual
return of the salmon and the trout; the seasonal and
geographic variations in the runs of the different
species determined the movements of the largely
nomadic tribes. Fish constituted a major part of the
Indian diet, was used for commercial purposes, and
indeed was traded in substantial volume. The Indians
developed food-preservation techniques that enabled
them to store fish throughout the year and to transport
it over great distances. They used a wide variety of
methods to catch fish including the precursors of all
modern netting techniques. Their usual and accustomed fishing places were numerous and were scattered throughout the area, and included marine as
well as fresh-water areas.*[2]

Indians have a right to take a considerable amount of fish
and game. However, tens of thousands of non-Indians now
want these same resources, both for sport and commercial
purposes. This has led to intense conflict. Indeed, few areas of
Indian law have created more conflict between Indians and
non-Indians than Indian hunting, fishing, and gathering rights.

Treaties and laws that guarantee Indian hunting and fishing
rights have been interpreted by the courts to include gathering
and trapping rights for those tribes that relied on these methods for obtaining their food. Many tribes gather berries, nuts,
or wild rice as an important part of their diet. Throughout this
chapter, references to hunting and fishing rights also generally
refer to gathering and trapping rights.

Which tribes still have hunting and fishing rights?

Every Indian tribe has the inherent right to be self-governing. This means, among other things, that every tribe has the right to regulate its land and resources, including the taking of wildlife. As explained in chapter 6, a tribe's governing powers can be limited by Congress, but until this occurs, an Indian tribe essentially retains all of its original rights. Obviously, one of its original rights was to hunt and fish within the territory it controlled.[3]

The right to hunt and fish was expressly guaranteed to many tribes in their treaties with the United States. However, this right is presumed to exist even if the treaty does not mention it. As the Supreme Court explained in 1905, a treaty is not a grant of rights to the Indians but a taking of rights from them. Consequently, if a treaty is silent on the subject of Indian hunting and fishing rights, then these rights are not limited by the treaty and still exist in full force. This same rule applies to tribes that were forced to move from their original homelands. Once a reservation is created for an Indian tribe, the tribe can exercise its hunting and fishing rights even if the reservation does not include any of the tribe's former homelands.

Congress has the power to eliminate Indian hunting and fishing rights. However, a court will not find that Congress has removed ("extinguished") these vital rights unless Congress has clearly stated an intention to do so. Any unclear language in a treaty or statute will be interpreted in favor of the Indians. This is one of the most important court-made rules concerning Indian rights.

Is the tribe entitled to compensation when Congress extinguishes its hunting and fishing rights?

Yes. The Fifth Amendment to the Constitution requires the federal government to pay compensation whenever it takes private property. The Supreme Court has held that Indian hunting and fishing rights are "property" protected by the Fifth Amendment. Any removal or destruction of this property by Congress entitles the tribe to compensation.

Does it violate the Constitution to give Indians special hunting and fishing rights?

No. As explained in chapter 5, Congress is authorized by the U.S. Constitution to treat Indians as a unique and separate political group. Congress is permitted to give Indians special rights as well as special burdens, and this includes access to wildlife that is denied to non-Indians.

Do hunting and fishing rights belong to the tribe or to the tribe's members as individuals?

In most situations, it makes no difference whether the right to hunt and fish is viewed as a tribal right or as an individual right. If a state law, for instance, is interfering with a tribe's treaty rights, both the tribe and its members can file suit to prevent enforcement of the law.

Indian hunting and fishing rights ultimately belong to the tribe. Tribal members can hunt and fish only to the extent allowed by the tribe. Likewise, if Congress takes away these rights and must then pay compensation, the money goes to the tribe, and the tribe decides what to do with it.

Can Indian tribes use hunting and fishing methods that did not exist when their treaties were signed?

Yes. The right to hunt and fish carries with it the right to use modern techniques for obtaining wildlife. A tribe that fished from the shore when its treaty was written can today use motorized boats to catch fish.

The right to hunt and fish also includes the right to take

wildlife that was not readily available when the reservation was created. A tribe that once hunted bison is entitled to hunt deer in exercising its treaty rights.

In exercising its hunting and fishing rights, a tribe is limited only by two rules, other than those it creates for itself. First, the tribe cannot take so much wildlife that it endangers continuation ("propagation") of the species in violation of state or federal conservation laws. Second, it cannot take any wildlife that Congress has expressly prohibited it from taking. (Both of these limitations are discussed later in this chapter.)

ON-RESERVATION HUNTING AND FISHING

Many Indian reservations are located in unpopulated areas of the United States where fish and game are plentiful. This wildlife provides food for tribal members and also offers an opportunity for commercial and sport hunting and fishing.

Most tribes that have wildlife on their reservations have created licensing and conservation programs and carefully manage their resources. Many tribes have found it profitable to develop a fish and game industry and sell licenses to non-Indians. In 1966, for instance, the Mescalero Apache Tribe in New Mexico had only thirteen elk on its reservation. The National Park Service donated 162 elk to the tribe. By 1983, the tribe had increased its herd to 1,200 and began issuing hunting licenses to nonmembers. The tribe also built a motel and restaurant, and now has a profitable tourist business.

There are three groups of people who may want to hunt or fish on an Indian reservation: tribal members, nonmembers who live on the reservation, and nonmembers who live off the reservation. There also are three governments that conceivably could exercise some authority over hunting and fishing on an Indian reservation: the tribe, the state, and the United States. The jurisdiction that each government has over these three groups is discussed later in this chapter.

To what extent can the tribe regulate on-reservation hunting and fishing?

Indian tribes have the power to manage the use of their land and the resources found on or in the land. This includes the power to regulate hunting and fishing by members and non-members on tribal lands and to prohibit all such activity if the tribe wants to. Only Congress has the authority to limit these tribal powers, and it rarely has done so.

Hunting and fishing is taken very seriously on most reservations because it is important to the economic, cultural, and religious heritage of the tribe. Many tribal members depend upon wildlife for food. In addition, some tribes obtain a large portion of their revenue through the sale of hunting and fishing licenses and from the resulting tourism. Accordingly, most tribes strictly regulate the time, place, and manner of hunting and fishing, and they enforce these rules through the tribal courts. Congress has strengthened the tribes' powers by making it a federal crime to hunt or fish on tribal land without the tribe's permission.

Thus, as a general rule, Indian tribes can regulate all hunting and fishing within the reservation. In *Montana v. United States* (1981), however, the Supreme Court created a significant exception to this rule. Tribes have limited powers, the Court held, to regulate non-Indian hunting and fishing on *non-Indian–owned* land within the reservation. (As explained in chapter 5, many non-Indians have purchased land on Indian reservations.) In these situations, the Court said, the tribe can impose its laws only when the activity would seriously hurt the tribe or its members. Otherwise, state law rather than tribal law governs non-Indian hunting and fishing on non-Indian land. For example, if non-Indians take so many fish and game from their own lands that tribal members cannot get enough to eat, the tribe can limit this activity, but in most other situations, it cannot.

To what extent can the state regulate on-reservation hunting and fishing?

A state cannot enforce its laws on an Indian reservation if that enforcement would violate federal law or would interfere with tribal self-government, unless Congress has given its consent. Congress has not consented to the enforcement of state game laws on Indian reservations. Even Public Law 83-280, which allows some states to prosecute crimes committed on the reservation, expressly withheld state jurisdiction over Indian hunting and fishing.

State regulation of reservation Indian hunting and fishing always interferes with tribal self-government. In addition, such regulation often violates Indian treaties, many of which guarantee that the tribe will remain free of state control. Therefore, these Indian activities cannot be regulated by the state. The only exception to this rule, and it is a narrow one, was created in *Puyallup Tribe, Inc. v. Department of Game* (1968). The Supreme Court held in *Puyallup* that a state can regulate reservation Indian fishing in the interest of conservation, that is, when necessary to ensure that enough fish escape to propagate the species. The measures that a state can and cannot take in the interest of conservation are discussed later in this chapter.

The state has no jurisdiction over hunting and fishing on *Indian* lands, even when non-Indians are involved. In *New Mexico v. Mescalero Apache Tribe* (1983), the Supreme Court ruled 9–0 that states may not exercise even concurrent (shared) jurisdiction over non-Indians who hunt or fish on tribal lands. Instead, tribal law controls. Thus, non-Indians who want to hunt or fish on tribal lands need not purchase a state license, but only a tribal license. Likewise, tribal law and not state law governs when and how hunting and fishing can occur, and how many fish and game can be taken.

There is one narrow exception to this rule. If a state can show that an animal is in danger of extinction, the state can impose its conservation measures on Indian land. But even here, the state may not automatically intervene. On the contrary, it may do so only if the tribe and the federal government do not already have adequate conservation plans of their own.

In sum, the state's authority regarding on-reservation hunting and fishing is limited to the situations discussed in *Montana v. United States* and *Puyallup*. First, the state can regulate non-Indians who hunt and fish on their own land. Second, the state can regulate Indians when this is essential for conservation purposes.

To what extent can the federal government regulate on-reservation hunting and fishing?

Federal officials have no authority on an Indian reservation except what Congress has expressly given them. Courts have held, for example, that without express congressional consent, federal officials may not tax reservation Indian hunting and fishing, or take any action that violates Indian treaty rights to hunt or fish. In addition, federal agencies may not build dams or authorize development projects by other persons that would hurt Indian hunting and fishing.

Federal officials, though, have been given three important duties by Congress. First, federal officials are required to help tribes enforce tribal law. Congress has made it a federal crime to hunt or fish on an Indian reservation in any manner that violates tribal law. Congress has also made it a federal crime to transport, sell, receive, or purchase any fish or wildlife in violation of tribal law. In other words, a violation of a tribal game law is automatically a violation of federal law. This is particularly important because in 1978 the Supreme Court held that non-Indians who violate tribal law cannot be prosecuted by the tribe. Now, every person who violates tribal game laws can be prosecuted by the federal government, including members of the tribe.

Second, federal officials have been authorized by Congress to file suit on behalf of Indian tribes to protect the tribe's treaty rights to hunt and fish, and many suits have been filed. Lastly, federal officials have been directed by Congress to issue regulations designed to conserve tribal fish or wildlife when the tribe's conservation measures have not worked (but this is rarely necessary). For the most part, on-reservation hunting and fishing remain entirely a matter of tribal regulation.

OFF-RESERVATION HUNTING AND FISHING

What kinds of off-reservation hunting and fishing rights do Indians have?

Many Indians have a federally protected right to hunt and fish outside the reservation. Indians have obtained these rights in two ways. On occasion, Congress has reduced the size of an Indian reservation, or even eliminated it, without removing the tribe's hunting and fishing rights on that land. Therefore, these rights remain.

On other occasions, Congress has expressly given a tribe the right to hunt or fish outside its reservation. Some tribes have a treaty right to hunt and fish "on the unoccupied and unclaimed lands of the United States," or something similar to this. Members of these tribes therefore have the right to hunt and fish on unsettled federal lands, such as areas within a national forest where hunting and fishing is otherwise restricted or prohibited.

A typical off-reservation right—and the one that has created the most controversy—is the fishing right. In treaties with tribes in Oregon and Washington, for example, it was a common practice for a tribe to give away most of its homelands in exchange for the right to fish "at all usual and accustomed grounds and stations," both on and off the reservation. Unfortunately, none of the treaties identified the exact location of any of these sites. In interpreting these treaties, federal courts have defined "usual and accustomed grounds and stations" as being all those locations where members of a tribe customarily fished at or before the time the treaty was signed. Proving where these sites are located is sometimes difficult, but dozens of locations have now been identified, and treaty tribes today are exercising their fishing rights at these locations. Some locations are far from the tribe's reservation. One tribe proved that it customarily fished forty miles out to sea, which was quite a feat, given the fishing vessels they had.

Non-Indians usually oppose the designation of an area as a traditional Indian fishing ground. There are several reasons why. First, many non-Indians fish for sport, and the more fish that Indians take, the fewer are available for sport. Second, many of these traditional sites are along riverbanks, where the Indians caught the adult fish returning to spawn. If the particular area where the fishing took place is now privately owned by a non-Indian, tribal members retain their right to fish there whether the owner consents or not.

The biggest reason is money. The fishing industry in the Northwest is a multimillion-dollar business, and Indians compete with non-Indians for the profits. One way non-Indians try to limit Indian fishing is by reducing the number of their federally protected sites, thereby making it more difficult for Indians to catch their share of the fish.

Tribes have every reason to assert their treaty rights: they gave up a large amount of land in exchange for these rights, and the United States should keep its end of the bargain. Keeping these off-reservation sites was of primary concern to the treaty tribes. As the Supreme Court has stated about the Northwest treaties:

All of the treaties were negotiated by Isaac Stevens, the first Governor and first Superintendent of Indian Affairs of the Washington Territory, and a small group of advisors. Contemporaneous documents make it clear that these people recognized the vital importance of the fisheries to the Indians and wanted to protect them from the risk that non-Indian settlers might seek to monopolize their fisheries. There is no evidence of the precise understanding the Indians had of any of the specific English terms and phrases in the treaty. It is perfectly clear, however, that the Indians were vitally interested in protecting their right to take fish at usual and accustomed places, whether on or off the reservations, and that they were invited by the white negotiators to rely and in fact did rely heavily on the good faith of the United States to protect that right.[4]

The government agents who wrote these treaties wanted to protect Indian fisheries. But their promise to do so was easy to make at the time; few non-Indians lived in that area of the country, and the fish supply seemed inexhaustible. Today the demand for fish is much greater than the supply. Many non-Indians are very angry about Indian treaty rights. Indeed, there have been so many examples of state officials and state residents violating Indian fishing rights that the Supreme Court warned in 1989 that it is willing to use "stern measures" to protect these rights.[5] This can include fining or jailing state officials who fail to protect Indian rights.

To what extent may the tribe regulate Indian hunting and fishing outside the reservation?

Tribal law usually does not apply outside the reservation; state law does. However, if a tribe has the right to engage in an off-reservation activity, the tribe can regulate tribal members' participation in that activity. Thus, if a tribe has a federal right to fish outside the reservation, the tribe can decide which members can exercise that right, and when and how they may do it. Members who violate these regulations can be arrested and prosecuted by the tribe.

To what extent can the state regulate Indian hunting and fishing outside the reservation?

As just explained, the state has complete authority to regulate Indian hunting and fishing off the reservation unless the Indian is exercising a federal right. By virtue of the Supremacy Clause in the U.S. Constitution, a federal right is superior to a state right when the two conflict.[6] Therefore, those tribes that have a federal right to hunt or fish off-reservation normally need not comply with state law. A state law, for instance, that limits people to catching three fish a day cannot be applied to an Indian exercising a federal right to fish.

Yet even here, the state has some control. There are two narrow but important exceptions to the rule that a state may not regulate off-reservation Indian rights. These exceptions are best illustrated by the court decisions interpreting the Northwest Indian treaties.

Almost all the treaties with Northwest tribes contain the

same two clauses, one of which already has been discussed. These treaties guarantee the Indians "the right of taking fish at all usual and accustomed grounds and stations . . . in common with all citizens of the Territory." As previously explained, the "grounds and stations" clause guarantees that the tribe may fish at all of its traditional locations, free from state interference. However, the "in common with" clause, the courts have held, gives the state some regulatory authority over these off-reservation rights.

The treaties do not explain what this clause means. Can the Indians, for example, take more than 5 percent of the fish if they represent only 5 percent of the population?

The Supreme Court has defined the "in common with" clause to mean that Indians have a right to take a certain portion of the fish and not just a right to cast a fishing line along with the tens of thousands of non-Indians who now fish in the area. The treaties did not simply guarantee Indians an opportunity to fish. They reserved to them a certain percentage of the catch. As a result, the state must prevent non-Indians from taking too many fish.

But non-Indians have rights, too. The "in common with" clause not only gives Indians a right to a certain amount of fish, the Supreme Court said, but it also gives non-Indians a right to the remainder. "Both sides have a right, secured by treaty, to take a fair share of the available fish. That, we think, is what the parties to the treaties intended when they secured to the Indians the right of taking fish in common with other citizens."[7]

In *Washington v. Washington State Commercial Passenger Fishing Vessel Association* (1979), the Supreme Court interpreted the "in common with" clause in specific terms. Indian tribes that have the right to fish "in common with other citizens of the Territory" may take up to 50 percent of the available fish, unless a lesser amount would provide the Indians with "a moderate living." The Court did not describe what exactly is a moderate living.

Using the Court's "moderate living" standard, there are four possible situations that can arise, and three have occurred. The first possibility is that the state must prevent the tribe from taking its entire 50 percent share because otherwise the tribe's income would exceed a moderate level. There are no court cases indicating that this situation has ever occurred. Few tribes have the money to buy enough boats and modern equipment to enable them to catch their share. As tribes get more money, this first possibility may occur.

The second possibility is that the state must prevent non-Indians from taking so many fish that Indians are unable to catch their 50 percent share. This situation happens often.

The third possibility is that, even if the tribe takes its 50 percent, this still is not enough to give them a moderate living because there is simply not enough fish. This is the situation in northern Wisconsin. Thus far, the federal courts in Wisconsin have not permitted the tribes to take more than 50 percent of the resource even though the Indians are not earning a moderate living.

The fourth possibility, which occurs infrequently, is that non-Indians fail to take their 50 percent of the wildlife. In that event, Indians are permitted to take more than their treaty share rather than waste the available resource.

In short, the general rule is that a state may not interfere with Indian treaty rights to hunt and fish, even off the reservation. There are two exceptions to this rule. One is the "moderate living" exception, just discussed. The second exception is that a state can limit Indian activities in the interest of conservation. But even here, the state's authority is limited. In order to be valid, the state must prove that its regulation is necessary to perpetuate the species, and that the regulation does not discriminate against Indians by preventing them from taking their treaty share of the resource.

To illustrate, a state can require tribes to issue identification cards to their members so that state officials can identify the Indians who have treaty rights. A state can also allow non-Indians to fish at a protected Indian site provided that tribal members have the opportunity to catch their treaty share of fish. A state can also prohibit Indians from taking fish that are near extinction provided that the same rule applies to non-Indians.

On the other hand, restrictions on Indians that are unnecessary or discriminatory are invalid. A state must not prevent the tribe from taking its fair share of treaty wildlife unless absolutely necessary to preserve the species. For example, a regulation that prohibits both Indians and non-Indians from using fishing nets may seem reasonable and fair. But if it prevents Indians from obtaining their 50 percent share of fish—and Indians probably cannot catch their treaty share unless nets are used—it discriminates against Indians and violates federal law. Likewise, treaty Indians are not required to obey state regulations on the number of fish they can take or the seasons in which they can fish unless absolutely necessary for conservation.

To what extent can the federal government regulate off-reservation Indian hunting and fishing?

If it wanted to, Congress could regulate every aspect of Indian hunting and fishing. Congress could even extinguish these treaty rights at any time, provided that it paid compensation to the tribe.

However, regulation of off-reservation Indian hunting and fishing rights has been left by Congress primarily in the hands of the tribes; federal officials have been given little authority to regulate them. The secretary of the interior has issued rules on the identification of treaty Indians and their gear and has regulated fishing activities at certain protected locations. In addition, Congress has passed a comprehensive law governing all fishing on the high seas within 200 miles of the coast, but federal officials are required by its terms to enforce this law consistent with Indian treaty rights. Thus, federal officials have little control over Indian hunting and fishing rights, other than their obligation, previously discussed, to help tribes enforce tribal hunting and fishing laws.

12

INDIAN WATER RIGHTS

Water is a scarce resource in most of the United States. In many parts of the West, where most Indians live, groundwater is now being consumed faster than it is being replenished. (Groundwater, as its name suggests, is water within the earth that supplies wells and springs.) Unless water is obtained from distant sources, or water-conservation measures are imposed, many western wells will run dry; some are dry already.

The Supreme Court has recognized that Indian tribes have the right to use a considerable amount of water. For good reason, tribes are very concerned about preserving and defending these water rights.

What is the *Winters* doctrine?

The most important case in Indian water law is *Winters v. United States*, decided by the Supreme Court in 1908. The issue in *Winters* was whether a landowner could dam a stream on his property, thereby preventing water from reaching an Indian reservation located downstream. The reservation had been created by Congress eight years before the landowner had purchased his property, and this stream supplied much of the tribe's water. However, the federal statute that created the reservation made no mention of water rights. The landowner therefore argued that the tribe was not entitled to water from that stream, and he was free to use all of the water himself.

The Supreme Court ruled in favor of the tribe. The reservation was arid and of little value without irrigation. Congress must have intended, the Court said, to reserve to the Indians enough water to irrigate their lands and make the reservation livable and productive. The Court ruled that Congress has the power to reserve water for federal lands, and by implication it exercises this power every time it creates an Indian reservation. Therefore, a sufficient amount of water had to reach the reservation to fulfill the purpose for which it was created. The Court ordered the landowner to dismantle the dam.

The *Winters* doctrine, also known as the "implied reservation of water" doctrine, has been consistently upheld by the Supreme Court. In a 1963 case, for example, the Court had to decide whether an Indian tribe was entitled to enough water to irrigate its entire reservation, even though part of the reservation had never been irrigated. The presidential order that created the reservation was silent on the subject of water rights. Citing *Winters*, the Court said that whenever an Indian reservation is created, there is an "implied reservation of water rights . . . necessary to make the reservation livable."[1] The tribe was entitled to an amount of water, the Court held, that would "satisfy the future as well as the present needs of the Indian reservation," that is, the amount necessary "to irrigate all the practicably irrigable acreage on the reservation."[2]

The basic principles of the *Winters* doctrine are as follows.

1. Congress has the right to reserve water for federal lands. Whenever Congress sets aside land for a specific purpose—

whether it be a national park, a military base, or an Indian reservation—it reserves by implication a sufficient quantity of water to fulfill that purpose.

2. Indian reservations are created by Congress with the purpose of making them livable and productive. Therefore, each Indian reservation is presumed to have a right to enough water to satisfy that goal—that is, enough water to meet the tribe's present *and* future needs.

What gives Congress the power to reserve water for Indians?

Article I, section 8, clause 3 of the Constitution (the Commerce Clause) gives Congress the power to regulate commerce with the Indian tribes. This clause gives Congress complete authority over Indian affairs, the Supreme Court has held, including the authority to give water rights to Indians.

What is the doctrine of prior appropriation?

As white settlers moved westward during the 1800s and bought homesteads, they quickly developed rules to govern the allocation of water. Without these rules they would have engaged in endless warfare over this scarce resource. The rules they developed, known as the "doctrine of prior appropriation," have been written into law in every western state.

This doctrine has four basic principles. The first principle is "first in time, first in right." That is, the first person who uses water from a water source (the person with the earliest "priority date") has a continuing right to use the same amount of water from the same source, and subsequent appropriators ("junior interests") can only use whatever remains. Second, these water rights are property rights. They belong to the owner entirely separate from the land, and thus they can be sold with the land or separately. Third, in times of scarcity the person with the earliest priority date may use his or her entire water entitlement, even if no water remains for junior interests. Finally, these water rights are forfeited if unused for a significant period of time.

To illustrate these principles, assume that Mr. A and Ms. B live along the same stream, and Ms. C lives behind Mr. A. In 1990, Mr. A begins taking 2,000 gallons of water a year from the stream, and he is the first person to take water from this stream. He registers his water use under state law, as required. The next year, Ms. B takes 2,000 gallons from the stream, and she also registers her water use. By making the first diversion, Mr. A has a priority date that is senior to Ms. B's. In times of drought, he can take his entire 2,000 gallons even if nothing remains for Ms. B. If ten years later Mr. A sells his water rights to Ms. C, she would acquire his priority date and all of his rights (even if her property does not touch the stream).

How does the *Winters* doctrine differ from the doctrine of prior appropriation?

Indian water rights (*Winters* rights) differ from rights under the doctrine of prior appropriation in three significant respects. First, *Winters* rights are federal rights, while appropriative rights are acquired under state law. Federal rights are always superior to state rights when the two conflict. Therefore, a state cannot limit a tribe's *Winters* water rights unless Congress has given its consent. For example, a state could not pass a law—as many states would like to—that reduces a tribe's *Winters* rights.

Second, Indian water rights are "reserved." A tribe cannot lose its *Winters* rights through nonuse, as is the case under state water law (the doctrine of prior appropriation). This is very important because many tribes have not had the money to use all of their water rights, and they would have lost them by now had these rights not been reserved.

Lastly, the amount of water a tribe is entitled to use is not determined by the tribe's initial use, as is true under state water law. On the contrary, a tribe with *Winters* rights is entitled to take all the water it needs to fulfill the purpose for which its reservation was created. Therefore, a tribe that currently is using only 2,000 gallons of water from a stream can take more in the future as its population grows or because it has begun to use additional water for agricultural or other purposes.

The *Winters* doctrine and the doctrine of prior appropriation do have one thing in common. Both provide that a senior interest (someone with an earlier priority date) has the right to use his or her entire entitlement even if no water remains for a junior interest. Thus, in the example used earlier, if an Indian reservation was created by Congress after Mr. A had registered his entitlement to water, the tribe would of course have *Winters* rights, but its rights would be junior to Mr. A's water rights. In the West, most Indian reservations were created before non-Indians acquired much land in the region. Therefore, Indian water rights usually have an early priority date—the date the reservation was created—and thus they are very valuable.

Indians enjoy the best of both worlds when it comes to water rights. The appropriation doctrine protects Indians even though they are not bound by its limitations. It protects them by making sure that junior interests take none of the water Indians need. Yet Indians are exempt from its rule that current (and future) water use is limited to initial water use and that water rights can be forfeited by nonuse. Indians can even increase their initial water use because Congress has reserved for them a sufficient quantity of water to meet their present and their future needs.

An Indian tribe, consistent with the doctrine of prior appropriation, has no obligation to share its water with any junior interest. In a time of drought, a tribe, like any other senior interest, has the right to use its full allocation of water even if non-Indians are left with an insufficient supply.

Which water laws govern the use of water in the eastern states?

The eastern states get more rainfall than the western states, and they developed a different set of laws governing the use of water. Eastern states rely on the "riparian doctrine." This doctrine distributes water more proportionally than the doctrine of prior appropriation. Under the riparian doctrine, prior use does not create a right to continued use, and in times of scarcity, the available water supply is distributed equitably among all users.

In states governed by the riparian doctrine, Indian reservations presumably have the same *Winters* rights as they do in the West. But this issue has never been litigated, probably because eastern reservations usually have an adequate water supply.

Can a tribe exercising its *Winters* rights use subsurface water as well as surface water?

Yes. *Winters* rights apply to surface water, including lakes, rivers, and streams, and to groundwater, including all aquifers that run under the reservation. (An aquifer is a water-bearing stratum of rock, sand, or gravel.) Tribes have a right to protect the availability of both sources of water, ground and surface.

Often, surface and subsurface water are linked. To illustrate, taking water from a well could cause a lake miles away to recede, if both are fed by the same aquifer. As a result, Indian tribes can prevent junior interests located off the reservation from using water (whether surface or ground) in any amount that depletes the tribe's *Winters* rights.

How much water is an Indian reservation entitled to use?

The short answer to this question is that a tribe is entitled to use as much water as is necessary to fulfill the purpose of the reservation once senior claims, if there are any, have taken their entitlement. However, this short answer involves two complicated inquiries: (1) What is the *purpose* of the reservation, and (2) Precisely what *quantity* of water is needed to fulfill that purpose?

1. Purpose. The basic purpose for which all Indian reservations are created is to serve as a permanent and economically viable home for the Indians who live there. Therefore, every Indian reservation is entitled to enough water to meet that goal.

However, calculating how much water a tribe is entitled to use requires that the reservation's purpose be identified in more specific terms. Is the purpose to grow crops, or to maintain fish and game, or perhaps to mine coal? What if the original purpose was to allow the tribe to fish from a river, but this river was recently dammed by the federal government for flood control, and few fish are left? The courts that have wrestled with these issues have recognized that tribes are permitted to obtain a sufficient amount of water to satisfy any reasonable purpose, taking into account the tribe's historical use of water, the intentions of those who created the reservation, and the tribe's need to maintain itself under changed circumstances.

2. Quantity. The Supreme Court has held that Indian tribes are entitled to a sufficient quantity of water to fulfill the purpose of the reservation. This quantity will differ from one reservation to another. A tribe that grows crops is likely to need more water than a tribe that raises cattle.

The Court has also held that a tribe's *Winters* rights do not extend beyond this. The *Winters* doctrine "reserves only that amount of water necessary to fulfill the purpose of the reservation, no more."[3] Moreover, in an Indian fishing-rights case, the Supreme Court held that "Indian treaty rights to a natural resource . . . secures so much as, but not more than, is necessary to provide the Indians with a livelihood—that is to say, a moderate living."[4]

Assuming that the Court would apply the "moderate living" standard to this context, the *Winters* doctrine reserves to the tribe and its members enough water to make them economically self-sufficient but not enough to make them rich. Calculating the precise quantity of water that is needed to achieve this purpose is no easy task, as explained later in this chapter.

Can the tribe put water to a different use than what Congress originally intended?

Yes. The only restriction on *Winters* rights is that the tribe use no more water than is necessary to satisfy the purpose of the reservation. How it uses this water is for the tribe to decide.

To be meaningful, Indian rights under the *Winters* doctrine must be flexible and accommodate change. If reservations are to serve as permanent homes, Indians must be allowed to shift their water use as their needs change and as technology develops. Water that Congress might have intended for agricultural use a century ago can be used for industrial development today.

Is water reserved for the tribe's recreational and environmental needs?

Yes. Under the *Winters* doctrine, every reserve of federal land, including an Indian reservation, is entitled to enough water to fulfill the purpose for which it was created. The purpose of every Indian reservation is to serve as a permanent and viable home for the Indians who live there. This purpose cannot be fulfilled unless the reservation offers recreational opportunities and a decent, hospitable environment. Therefore, a tribe with *Winters* rights is entitled to enough water to satisfy its recreational and environmental needs. If a tribe wishes to build a community swimming pool or if tribal members want to water their lawns, they have a right under the *Winters* doctrine to use water for these purposes.

Are Indian tribes using the full amount of their *Winters* rights? If not, who is using the remainder?

There may not be a single tribe currently using its entire *Winters* entitlement of water. Money is the main reason. Many tribes, for instance, have the right to irrigate their entire reservation, but few of them can afford the irrigation systems necessary to do so.

Whenever a tribe is not using its entire entitlement of water, the tribe can sell the excess to the highest bidder. But before it can do this, the tribe needs to know *exactly* how much water it is entitled to obtain under the *Winters* doctrine. In other words, its rights must be *quantified*.

Assume, for example, that a stream runs through an Indian reservation (as is true for many reservations). Each year, 20 million gallons of water flow down the stream, of which the tribe uses one million. The rest flows downstream. Can the tribe sell any of the rest, rather than let the downstream users take it for free?

Obviously, the tribe cannot sell the water unless it first knows how much of the 20 million gallons it has a right to take. If the tribe has a right to take all of it, it can sell the 19 million gallons it is not currently using. On the other hand, if it only

151

has a right to use one million gallons, it must allow the rest of the water to pass through the reservation.

Quantifying a tribe's *Winters* rights is time-consuming and expensive. It is a two-step process. First, the purpose of the reservation must be determined. Second, experts must calculate how much water is needed to fulfill that purpose.

If the purpose of a reservation is agricultural, then the tribe is entitled to enough water to irrigate all the "practicably irrigable acreage" (PIA) on the reservation.[5] PIA has two components: the land must be of sufficient quality to grow crops, and the cost of supplying water to that land must not be unreasonable. (In other words, a tribe would not be allowed enough water to irrigate a desert because doing that is not practicable.) Determining the amount of water these tribes are entitled to use is not an easy task. Experts must determine what kind of crops (if any) can be grown on each parcel of reservation land and then calculate how much water is necessary to grow those crops.

Similar difficulties exist for those tribes dependent on hunting and fishing. These tribes are entitled to enough water to maintain the lakes, streams, or forests where their fish and game are found, but quantifying this precise amount of water is very difficult. (Indian reservations that were created for both purposes—growing crops and taking wildlife—are entitled to water for both purposes.)

From the tribe's perspective, there are advantages and disadvantages to quantifying its water rights. The main advantage is that once its rights are quantified, the tribe can prevent junior interests from taking the tribe's water, and the tribe can begin to charge junior interests for using it. However, as explained earlier, tribes are permitted to increase their water usage if a change in circumstances requires it. Therefore, the disadvantage of quantification is that the tribe will be locked into a fixed entitlement that later may be inadequate. Moreover, quantification is expensive.

Likewise, there are advantages and disadvantages from the junior interests' perspective. The main advantage is that quantification eliminates uncertainty. This allows junior interests to plan for the future. Without quantification, the tribe's rights remain open-ended because no one knows what the tribe's future needs will be. The fact that tribes have open-ended rights has led to uncertainty and anger. Many non-Indian landowners are unable to expand their cattle herds, or develop their land, because they do not know how much water the tribe will claim in the future.

The disadvantage, though, is that junior interests may suddenly learn that the tribe's entitlement is so large that junior interests now must purchase water they had been taking for free. Some junior interests may be forced out of business once they must pay for water.

Most experts on this subject, including the National Water Commission, recommend that the United States assist tribes in quantifying their water rights so as to eliminate the uncertainty that is now plaguing western development. By far the best solution is for tribes and other water users to negotiate a fair division of the water, based on legal rights and needs. Litigating these cases in court can be very expensive (a recent Wyoming lawsuit cost $14 million), and lawsuits often cause bitterness that can be avoided through open negotiation. A number of tribes and their neighbors are now engaged in these negotiations.

Under what circumstances may a tribe regulate the use of water by a non-Indian?

In the *Winters* case, a tribe restricted a non-Indian's water use off the reservation. Non-Indians, both on and off the reservation, may not interfere with a tribe's senior right to reserved water.

Are Indian water rights protected by the Just Compensation Clause?

As explained in chapter 5, Indians and tribes are entitled to compensation whenever the federal government eliminates their vested property rights. This rule applies to Indian *Winters* rights, which are vested rights.

Does the federal government have an obligation to protect Indian water rights?

Yes. As discussed in chapter 3, the federal government has a responsibility to protect Indian property and to help tribes prosper. Water is essential to meeting this goal. Therefore, the federal government has an obligation, recognized in the *Winters* doctrine itself, of assuring adequate supplies of water to Indian reservations. The government is responsible for what happens to a tribe's *Winters* rights and can be sued by the tribe for mismanaging them.

Has the federal government made a good faith effort to protect Indian water rights?

Not always. As the National Water Commission stated in its 1973 report to Congress:[6]

> *During most of this 50-year period [following the Supreme Court's decision in the* Winters *case in 1908], the United States was pursuing the policy of encouraging the settlement of the West and the creation of family-sized farms on its arid lands. In retrospect, it can be seen that this policy was pursued with little or no regard for Indian water rights and the* Winters *doc-*

*trine. With the encouragement, or at least the coopera-
tion, of the Secretary of the Interior—the very office
entrusted with protection of all Indian rights—many
large irrigation projects were constructed on streams
that flowed through or bordered Indian reservations,
sometimes above and more often below the reservations. With few exceptions, the projects were planned
and built by the federal government without any
attempt to define, let alone protect, prior rights that
Indian tribes might have had in the waters used for
the projects. . . . In the history of the United States
Government's treatment of Indian tribes, its failure to
protect Indian water rights for use on the reservations
it set aside for them is one of the sorrier chapters.*

The federal government often has conflicts of interest
when it comes to water rights. It is obligated on one hand to
protect tribal rights. Yet it also has a continuing obligation to
maintain national parks and national forests, promote land
development, and to build dams for flood control, among other
responsibilities. Frequently, government agencies, when faced
with scarce water resources, ignore Indian water rights in
favor of other interests. As President Nixon admitted in 1970,
"There is considerable evidence that the Indians are the losers
when such situations arise."[7]

Tribes can file lawsuits to protect their water rights. Tribes
have obtained court orders halting a number of on- and off-
reservation activities that were depleting or polluting their
water. They have also been successful in forcing federal agencies to stop issuing permits to other water users where this
would result in a loss of tribal water. However, Congress has
removed water rights from a number of tribes, and tribes
always have to worry that being too aggressive could cause

Congress to take away tribal water. Even though Congress would then have to pay money compensation to the tribe for the value of the rights that were removed, the loss of water may prevent tribes from having any realistic chance of attaining self-sufficiency in the future.

13

CIVIL RIGHTS OF INDIANS

What is a civil right?

The citizens of every democratic society decide two things: what powers their government will have, and what individual rights citizens will have. These individual ("civil") rights guarantee basic freedoms, thereby protecting against government abuse.

Most of the civil rights that U.S. citizens have are set forth in the U.S. Constitution and in laws passed by Congress. State constitutions and state laws are additional sources of civil rights. The U.S. Constitution (and especially its first ten amendments, the Bill of Rights) guarantees numerous civil rights, including freedom of speech, press, and religion; protection against unreasonable search and seizure; protection against the loss of life or liberty without due process of law; and the right to bail, counsel, and a trial by jury. In addition to these constitutional rights, Congress has passed dozens of laws that create civil rights. These laws protect people from such things as racial or sexual discrimination in employment and housing; they protect the right to vote in state and federal

157

elections; and they ensure that disabled persons have the right to use federally funded programs.

Do Indians have the same civil rights as other citizens?

Yes. The Fourteenth Amendment to the U.S. Constitution guarantees that all citizens enjoy "equal protection of the laws," which means that all citizens must be treated equally under the law. In 1924 Congress declared that every Indian born in this country is a U.S. citizen.[1] Indians thus have the same civil rights as all other citizens.

This chapter does not try to explain the numerous civil rights that all citizens share. It would take many pages to do so. Instead, it focuses on those civil rights that are most important to Indians because of their culture, religion, or race. These rights have special meaning for Indians in their dealings with the state and federal governments. (Chapter 14 discusses civil rights with respect to tribal governments.)

FREEDOM OF RELIGION

Which provisions of the Constitution guarantee freedom of religion?

The U.S. Constitution contains two religion clauses, and both are found in the First Amendment: the Establishment Clause and the Free Exercise Clause. They read as follows: "Congress shall make no law respecting an establishment of religion or prohibiting the free exercise thereof."

Many Europeans who first settled in what is now the United States came here because they wanted freedom of religion. They were driven from their homelands because of their religious beliefs. In order to ensure religious freedom in this country, these clauses were placed into the Constitution.

What do the Establishment and Free Exercise Clauses guarantee?

The Establishment Clause assures that religion and government will remain separate ("the separation of church and state"). The government can neither promote nor inhibit religion. Instead, it must remain entirely neutral in religious matters. The Establishment Clause guarantees that no agency of government will meddle in religious affairs or engage in a religious activity.

The Free Exercise Clause guarantees individual freedom of worship. Religion in this country is a matter of private choice. As a result of this freedom to choose, there are more than 250 religions practiced in the United States.

Taken together, these clauses guarantee that each of us can believe in any religion we want, or in no religion (the Free Exercise Clause), and that no group, including the majority, can use the government to promote or hinder religion (the Establishment Clause). By guaranteeing that religion and government will be separate, and by protecting private religious activity, each of us is assured freedom of religion.

How have these clauses protected Indians?

Religion plays a major role in Indian life. For many Indians, everything we do and everything that exists in the world has religious significance. Therefore, the Constitution's guarantee of religious freedom and the separation of church and state have great importance for Indians.

Until recently, the Free Exercise Clause was particularly important. Courts had interpreted this clause as requiring the government to prove that a "compelling interest" exists before the government could undertake an action that interfered with religion or with a religious practice. This is a heavy burden of proof. The government must have more than a rational reason for doing something that hurts religion; the reason must be compelling. To illustrate, let's say that the federal government wants to build a new highway, and there are two possible routes. One route is a little cheaper but it would require the destruction of a famous church located in its path. The government has a rational reason for choosing this route: it's cheaper. However, saving a little money is usually not a compelling reason sufficient to justify an action that hurts religion. In this case, therefore, the government would be required to spend more money and build the highway on the other route.

Under the "compelling interest" test, many people (non-Indians and Indians alike) were able to obtain an exemption from certain laws. For example, courts held that (1) children should be excused from public school on their religious holidays; (2) Indians who use peyote as a religious sacrament should be exempt from laws that make it a crime to possess peyote; and (3) Indian prisoners who keep their hair long for religious reasons should be exempt from prison regulations requiring all prisoners to have short hair. In each case, the government could not show a sufficiently compelling reason to override the religious interests at stake.

The Supreme Court, however, drastically narrowed the scope of the Free Exercise Clause in a series of cases beginning in 1986. The Court held that, in most situations, the government only has to show a rational reason for taking an action, even if the action harms religion by injuring a religious belief or practice. To illustrate, the Court held in one case that an Indian who, for religious reasons, refuses to obtain a Social Security number, can be denied Social Security benefits under a law that requires all citizens to have a number. In another case, the Court permitted the federal government to build a road through sacred Indian lands, even though an alternative route was available but slightly more expensive to build. In a third case, the Court allowed prison officials to force prisoners to work during the time when, according to their religion, they should be offering their prayers.

Numerous citizens were disappointed and outraged by these court decisions, and pressured Congress to pass a civil-rights law that would restore the "compelling interest" test to these situations. This effort succeeded. In 1993 Congress passed the Religious Freedom Restoration Act (RFRA),[2] which prohibited the government from restricting "a person's exercise of religion" unless the government action satisfies "a compelling governmental interest." However, in 1997, the Supreme Court held that RFRA was unconstitutional because Congress is not permitted to change a constitutionally required test. Now, only a constitutional amendment can change the test.

What is the American Indian Religious Freedom Act?

The compelling interest test, required by RFRA, is a "balancing" test. That is, a court must weigh two things, one against the other: the government's interest in undertaking the activity is balanced against the harm it will cause to an individual's (or group's) religion. A government activity that would cause great harm will be harder to justify than one that causes, say, only a minor inconvenience.

For Indians, the problem with this approach is that many non-Indians do not appreciate the importance of certain Indian religious beliefs and practices. To a non-Indian judge, a government activity may seem harmless, but to Indians, the consequences could be enormous. To illustrate, Devil's Tower is a large rock outcropping in Wyoming that has tremendous religious significance to certain Indian tribes. To some non-Indians, allowing people to climb this rock (and to place metal loops into the rock to assist the climbers) may seem insignificant. But to many Indians, it is as sacrilegious as it would be to Christians if someone drilled holes into a statue of Jesus

161

on the cross and climbed all over it just for sport.

In an effort to help Indians protect their religious sites and practices, Congress passed a Joint Resolution in 1978 known as the American Indian Religious Freedom Act (AIRFA).[3] As with all Joint Resolutions, AIRFA contains no penalty provision that can be enforced against violators. However, AIRFA declares a policy that Congress has pledged itself to pursue:

> *[H]enceforth it shall be the policy of the United States to protect and preserve for Native Americans their inherent right of freedom of belief, expression, and exercise of traditional religions of the American Indian . . . including but not limited to access to sites, use and possession of sacred objects, and the freedom to worship through ceremonials and traditional rites.*

AIRFA has not been very effective because it lacks a penalty provision. Despite AIRFA, government officials have taken many actions that harmed Indian religious sites and practices, such as building a dam, and in one case a ski resort, on sacred Indian lands. Many Indians have requested that Congress amend this law and add a penalty clause, but Congress has not done so.

In addition to the U.S. Constitution and RFRA, citizens have certain protections under state constitutions and laws regarding religious practices. The federal government is not the only source of civil rights in this area. Every state constitution guarantees the separation of church and state, and protects religious worship.

INDIANS AS STATE CITIZENS

What rights do Indians have as state citizens?

The Fourteenth Amendment guarantees that all citizens are entitled to "equal protection of the laws." This is known as the Equal Protection Clause of the Constitution. Among other things, the clause prohibits state officials from discriminating against any person on account of race, color, creed, sex, or religion. Any difference in treatment based on one of these factors is unconstitutional unless the state has a compelling interest that requires it.

Have state officials discriminated against Indians?

Yes, many times. Indians have had to go to court to secure their right to hold state public office, attend public schools, receive state public assistance, serve as jurors in state court, obtain state business licenses, and receive the same municipal services (such as roads, streetlights, and police protection) that other citizens receive. The U.S. Commission on Civil Rights concluded, after an investigation in South Dakota, that Indians as a group receive longer criminal sentences from state judges than whites who are convicted of the same crime.[4]

State officials have attempted to justify some of these inequities by pointing to the fact that Indians have special rights under federal treaties and laws and do not pay certain state taxes. These officials claim that Indians should not have all the benefits of state citizenship because they do not share all of the burdens.

True, Indians have special rights and receive special benefits from the federal government. But so do many other groups, and yet no one denies them the full rights of citizenship. Moreover, it is particularly unfair to label Indians as being "special citizens" when they are the most impoverished and disadvantaged group in our society. As one writer has stated on this subject:

Any American who has been on an Indian reservation knows very well that Indians are not "equal." The highest infant mortality rate and lowest life expectan-

cy in the country reflect massive unmet health needs. Family income is by far the lowest in the nation. Housing and education deficits are greater than in any other sector of our society.

The fact that Indians have some special treaty rights is perfectly consistent with our form of government. The essence of American democracy is to provide "special benefits." We have special benefits for veterans, the elderly, the infirm, elementary and secondary school students, small businessmen, laborers, non-English speaking minorities and uncounted others. In our system, equality is achieved by a melding of many special programs which are directed toward special groups.

Thus Indian treaty rights, which were paid for so dearly by the tribes, cannot fairly be isolated. It is ironic, and brutally so, that there are those who would claim that the Indians are "favored" or "more than equal."[5]

Many state officials, of course, do not discriminate against Indians. Some even discriminate in their favor. Indians often discriminate against non-Indians, too. Hopefully, Indians and non-Indians will make a determined effort to eliminate these barriers to true equality.

THE RIGHT TO VOTE

Is the right to vote protected by federal law?

Yes. The right to vote is the most basic civil right in a democracy because it is the primary means by which all other rights can be safeguarded.

The right to vote is protected by federal law. The Fifteenth Amendment to the Constitution guarantees that no citizen shall be denied the right to vote in a state or federal election on account of race. In addition, the Voting Rights Act of 1965 protects all persons from having to pay a fee or pass a literacy test in order to vote. It also prohibits discrimination against persons whose primary language is not English. Indians are expressly recognized in the act as a language minority group.

Have Indians been subjected to discrimination in exercising their voting rights?

Indians have been forced to go to court many times to protect their right to vote. However, it is now firmly established that Indians have the same right to vote that all other citizens have. Indians cannot be denied the right to vote in state elections simply because they are exempt from paying some state taxes, or because they live on an Indian reservation. In addition, the Voting Rights Act requires that, where necessary to facilitate voting rights, state election officials must place voter registration offices in Indian communities, distribute voting information in the local Indian language, and recruit bilingual election officials to serve in Indian districts.

In many areas of the country, Indians constitute a large portion of the population, and their votes can determine the outcome of an election. But many Indians fail to vote. As a result, Indians have much less political influence than they could have. Not only are they often unable to help decide who gets elected, but elected officials also tend to ignore Indian concerns. Indians could obtain a significant amount of power and influence if more Indians voted.

ELIGIBILITY FOR PUBLIC OFFICE

Do Indians have the right to hold public office?

Definitely. Prior to 1924, when Congress conferred citizenship on Indians, some federal and state statutes prohibited Indians from holding particular public offices. Today such statutes would clearly be found to violate the Fourteenth and Fifteenth Amendments to the Constitution. Indians cannot be denied public office on account of race, their exemption from paying certain taxes, or residence on an Indian reservation. Indians have the same right as non-Indians to hold public office.

PROTECTION AGAINST PRIVATE DISCRIMINATION

Do Indians have any protection against discrimination by private persons?

The civil rights that are guaranteed by the U.S. Constitution, including the Fourteenth Amendment's guarantee of equal protection, apply *only* to government activities. They offer no protection against purely private discrimination. Thus, if a grocery store, gas station, or restaurant refused to serve you because of your race or sex, the Constitution offers no remedy from such private activity.

During the past 50 years, Congress has passed a number of civil-rights laws that prohibit various forms of discrimination by one individual or group against another. Congress enacted these laws because many citizens were being denied basic necessities of life, such as housing and employment, on account of racial or other discrimination.

These laws protect all citizens, Indians and non-Indians alike. Therefore, if an Indian suffers discrimination on account of race, color, creed, religion, sex, or national origin with respect to housing, employment, commercial transactions, or access to public accommodations (such as restaurants and most other businesses), a lawsuit can be filed in federal court to halt this discrimination and to recover damages for any injury suffered as a result of it.

PROTECTION OF BURIAL REMAINS

What is the Native American Graves Protection and Repatriation Act?

An investigation conducted during the late 1980s revealed that hundreds of thousands of Indian human remains were held by federal agencies and private museums receiving federal funding. After a concerted effort by Indians and Indian organizations, Congress in 1990 enacted the Native American Graves Protection and Repatriation Act (NAGPRA).[6]

NAGPRA does four things. First, it requires federal agencies and private museums receiving federal funds to inventory their collections of Indian human remains and any related funeral objects. The tribe of origin, if known, must then be notified. If the tribe requests it, these objects must be returned. Second, NAGPRA declares that Indian tribes are the owners of human remains and cultural items excavated or discovered on federal or tribal land. Third, NAGPRA makes it a federal crime to sell or trade Indian human remains and funeral items unless obtained in compliance with the act. Finally, NAGPRA requires that federal agencies and private museums receiving federal funds must make an itemized list of their other Indian artifacts, and if a tribe can prove a right of possession, the object must be returned to the tribe upon request.

167

14

THE INDIAN CIVIL RIGHTS ACT

In 1968 Congress passed the Indian Civil Rights Act (ICRA). The ICRA is a very controversial law because it authorizes federal courts to intervene in a tribe's internal governmental disputes, a power they never had before. The ICRA is the only law ever passed by Congress that expressly limits the power of every tribe to regulate its internal affairs.

Essentially, the ICRA does two things. First, it confers certain rights on all persons who are subject to the authority of a tribal government. Second, it authorizes federal courts to determine whether a tribe has violated, or is violating, some of those rights. In other words, the ICRA allows an *outside* authority to overrule a tribe's decision in certain internal matters.

Why did Congress pass the Indian Civil Rights Act?

As explained in chapter 6, the Supreme Court decided cases during the 1800s that recognized the following three principles. First, Indian tribes have the inherent right to govern themselves. Second, even the U.S. Constitution does not limit the powers of an Indian tribe. In other words, Indian tribes can engage in activities that, if done by the federal or state government, would violate the Constitution. Third, the Constitution gives Congress the right to limit (and even abolish) a tribe's powers, but until Congress does, each tribe retains its inherent right to be self-governing.

These Supreme Court decisions had the effect of leaving internal (intratribal) disputes entirely in the hands of the tribe. Indians who felt mistreated by tribal officials had to resolve their complaints within the tribe; they could not look elsewhere for help, even to the federal courts.

In 1962 a subcommittee of the U.S. Senate began a series of hearings concerning the administration of law and justice by tribal governments. Hundreds of people testified. Many tribal members claimed that tribal officials were tyrannical and biased. They accused tribal officials, for example, of rigging tribal elections, of favoring friends and relatives in business transactions, of firing tribal employees who had supported their opponents in tribal elections, and of not providing in tribal criminal proceedings the basic protections of a fair trial.

Many tribal members requested that Congress pass legislation protecting them from further abuse. Other tribal members disputed the need for this sort of legislation and argued that federal meddling in tribal matters could destroy tribes. They claimed that these abuses were not occurring, and even if they were, tribes must be permitted to resolve these problems themselves.

The senators who heard this testimony were startled and disturbed to learn that the Constitution did not limit tribal powers. This meant that tens of thousands of U.S. citizens were living under a government that did not have to respect constitutional rights. As one senator stated on the floor of the Senate: "As the hearings developed and as the evidence and testimony were taken, I believe all of us who were students of the law were jarred and shocked by the conditions as far as constitutional rights for members of the Indian tribes were concerned. There was found to be unchecked and unlimited authority over many facets of Indian rights. . . . The Constitution simply was not applicable."[1]

The end result of these hearings was the passage of the Indian Civil Rights Act. The purpose of the ICRA is "to ensure that the American Indian is afforded the broad Constitutional rights secured to other Americans . . . [in order to] protect individual Indians from arbitrary and unjust actions of tribal governments."[2]

The Indian Civil Rights Act (Title 25, U.S. Code, Sections 1301–41) is divided into five parts, only one of which confers civil rights (Sections 1301–03). The other parts concern such matters as how a state can acquire or relinquish jurisdiction over an Indian reservation. (These subjects are discussed elsewhere in this book.)

What civil rights are conferred by the ICRA?

Most of the civil rights conferred by the U.S. Constitution are conferred by the ICRA. Thus, Indian tribes are prohibited by the ICRA from doing most of the things that the Constitution prohibits the federal and state governments from doing.

Some senators initially suggested that every constitutional right be included in the ICRA. It was pointed out, however, that certain provisions of the Constitution would seriously undermine, if not destroy, tribal government. For instance, if tribes had to comply with the Fifteenth Amendment, they could not discriminate in voting on account of race.[3] This would mean that non-Indians who lived on the reservation could vote in tribal elections and hold tribal office. On some reservations more non-Indians live there than Indians, and the reins of tribal government probably would change hands.

The Establishment Clause of the First Amendment presented another unique problem. That clause requires the federal and state governments to remain neutral in religious matters, not preferring one religion over another religion. If this provision was enforced on Indian reservations, it would interfere with those tribes in which religious leaders are automatically the leaders of government. (This form of government is known as a theocracy.)

As finally enacted, the ICRA confers every fundamental civil right in the Constitution except five. The ICRA does not contain an Establishment Clause, and it does not prevent a tribe from discriminating in voting on account of race. Tribes also are not required to convene a jury in civil trials. In addition, in criminal cases, tribes do not have to issue grand-jury indictments to start criminal proceedings but can use the simpler method of issuing an arrest warrant, and the tribe does not have to appoint an attorney for a criminal defendant who cannot afford to hire one. (The ICRA requires a tribe to allow a defendant to be represented by an attorney at his or her own expense. It does not require the tribe to hire one if the defendant cannot afford one, as is the rule in state and federal courts.) The main reason these last three constitutional guarantees were not imposed on tribes is because they are very expensive to implement, and Congress was worried that tribes could not afford them.

The rights conferred by the ICRA are listed in Section 1302 of the act, which is reprinted in appendix A. Among them are the right to free speech, press, and assembly; protection against unreasonable search and seizure; the right to a speedy trial; the right to hire a lawyer in a criminal case; protection against self-incrimination; protection against cruel and inhuman punishment; and the right to equal protection of the laws and to due process of law.

171

Does the ICRA protect non-Indians as well as Indians?

Yes. The ICRA expressly applies to "any person" who is subject to the authority of a tribal government.[4]

Does the ICRA limit the punishment that criminals can receive?

Yes. The ICRA limits tribal punishment in criminal cases to one year imprisonment or a $5,000 fine, or both.[5] A person who commits two crimes could receive two one-year sentences to be served consecutively.

Have tribes had to alter some of their institutions and practices because of the ICRA?

Yes. The ICRA requires all tribes to meet certain federal standards. In order to do so, a number of changes had to be made. Those tribes that did not have a system for setting reasonable bail and for issuing search warrants, and those tribal courts that did not always provide a speedy trial or a right to a jury trial in criminal cases, had to change. Some tribes had to change many practices, while other tribes were already meeting most, if not all, of the requirements in the ICRA.

If a tribe violates rights protected by the ICRA, what can be done about it? Can the tribe be sued?

Congress has passed more than 100 civil-rights laws. These laws give citizens, among other things, protection against race and sex discrimination in housing and employment. Each time Congress passes one of these laws, it usually authorizes federal courts to hear and decide cases in which a citizen claims a violation of that right.

The ICRA is an exception to the rule that a federal right will have a federal remedy. The ICRA confers in Section 1302 a long list of rights, but the remedy, which is set out in Section 1303, allows federal courts to enforce only a few of them. Section 1303 states: "The privilege of the writ of habeas corpus shall be available to any person, in a court of the United States, to test the legality of his detention by order of an Indian tribe." The fact is, many of the rights listed in Section 1302 cannot be enforced in this manner.

A writ of habeas corpus is a court order. It orders that a person being held in custody be brought before the court so that the court can determine whether the detention is illegal. Thus if you are being detained in a tribal jail in violation of the ICRA, you can petition a federal court for a writ of habeas corpus.

A writ of habeas corpus is available only to challenge a detention. It is therefore clear that some of the federal rights conferred by Section 1302 have no federal-court remedy. To illustrate, if a tribe takes your property without compensating you in violation of Section 1302(5), or if a tribe discriminates against you in employment in violation of 1302(8), the federal courts cannot intervene because no detention is involved.

In 1978, the Supreme Court confirmed in *Santa Clara Pueblo v. Martinez* that the writ of habeas corpus is the only remedy that federal courts can grant under the ICRA. Tribal officials are required to obey the entire ICRA, a federal law. However, federal courts may enforce the ICRA only when a detention is involved. In all other circumstances, the Court said, victims of ICRA violations must seek a remedy in a tribal forum, whether it be in the tribal courts, the tribal council, or by electing a different set of tribal leaders.

As a practical matter, this has meant that a remedy does not exist for many violations of the ICRA. Some tribes, for example, do not permit their courts to decide ICRA cases. On those reservations, someone in a minority political group has no realistic chance of voting tribal leaders out of office and therefore has no judicial or political forum in which to seek a remedy.

Should the ICRA be amended so as to permit broader federal court review?

Many tribal members have urged Congress to amend the ICRA to permit federal courts to hear every kind of ICRA case. Without this protection, they claim, the situation is nearly as bad as before the act was passed.

Even if abuses are still occurring, this does not mean that Congress should amend the ICRA and authorize federal courts to resolve all ICRA disputes. After all, many people in the United States feel that they lack any realistic remedy when state or federal officials violate some of their civil rights, but no one seriously suggests that another government, such as France or England, should resolve these controversies. Why, then, should the federal government meddle in tribal disputes?

There clearly are two sides to this argument. Those who oppose amending the ICRA emphasize that tribes have a right to govern themselves. If someone disagrees with a tribal decision, he or she should work within the tribal system to change it. Permitting outsiders to resolve tribal disputes, many of which concern tribal customs and traditions, could severely disrupt tribal government and Indian culture.

Those who favor amending the ICRA argue that ICRA violations, especially on certain reservations, are so flagrant and injurious that resort to a federal court is necessary if basic civil rights are to be respected. Moreover, the absence of an effective tribal remedy for these abuses is already undermining tribal government by creating disrespect for tribal law and tribal officials. Without a federal court "safety net," it is argued, reservation Indians are the only people in the United States whose fundamental civil liberties can be violated without the opportunity for federal court review.

A few years ago, the U.S. Commission on Civil Rights proposed what might be viewed as a middle ground in this controversy. The commission suggested that Congress appropriate sufficient funds to train tribal officials, especially tribal judges, in the proper administration of the ICRA. Congress, however, has not appropriated this money. As a result, the controversy continues to rage as to whether the ICRA should be amended to allow for greater federal court review of ICRA violations.

15

THE SPECIAL STATUS
OF CERTAIN INDIAN GROUPS

Certain Indian groups have a special status under United
States law. These groups include the Pueblos of New Mexico,
Alaska Natives, Oklahoma Indians, and the New York Indians.
This chapter discusses the federal government's unique rela-
tionship with each of these groups.

THE PUEBLOS OF NEW MEXICO

What is the historical background of the Pueblos of
New Mexico?

Native communities were well established in what is now New
Mexico long before the Spanish conquistadors entered the
region during the 1600s. Each community had its own government, language, and culture. Today there are nineteen of these
Pueblo tribes in New Mexico, and each one is different politically and culturally.

The Spaniards felt it was their duty to "civilize" the Indians.

To help accomplish this, they built a church in each pueblo and sent missionaries to convert the Indians to Catholicism. Spain also issued a land grant recognizing the Pueblo tribes' ownership of all the land surrounding the church for one league (approximately 2.5 miles) in every direction. Spain then made it illegal for non-Indians to live within the pueblo.

Mexico acquired this region when it gained its independence from Spain. The Mexican government recognized the land grants that Spain had given to these tribes and extended Mexican citizenship to their members. However, the Mexican government did little to protect the Pueblos from being attacked by outsiders, and many Pueblos lost some land during this period.

The United States acquired New Mexico in an 1848 treaty with Mexico, the Treaty of Guadalupe Hidalgo. In the treaty, the United States promised to preserve the land rights that Mexico had granted to the Pueblos. Soon afterward, Congress passed laws recognizing the land ownership rights of each Pueblo, and conferring United States citizenship on the Pueblo Indians.

For most of the next 60 years, the federal government did not keep its promise to protect the Pueblos. Once again, non-Indians stole their land. It was not until 1913 that the federal government officially recognized the Pueblos as Indian tribes eligible for federal protection, and federal officials began protecting them. In 1924, Congress helped the Pueblos recover some of their stolen lands by passing the Pueblo Lands Act. This law required that all former Pueblo land be returned unless the settler could prove continuous payment of state real estate taxes from the date the land was removed from Pueblo control. Many settlers who had stolen Pueblo land had not paid state taxes on it and had to return the land.

It is now well established that the United States has a trust relationship with each Pueblo. As explained in chapter 3, this means that the federal government has a duty to protect Pueblo lands, and the Pueblo Indians are entitled to the same benefits and services that other federally recognized tribes receive.

In what respects is the relationship between the federal government and the Pueblos unique?

The Pueblos have a unique relationship with the United States. No other group of Indians has been so free of federal interference as the Pueblos. Congress rarely intrudes into Pueblo life.

It is not clear why Congress has treated the Pueblos differently from other tribes. It may be a combination of several factors. First, the Pueblos own their land. On most other reservations, the land is owned in large part by the United States, and thus the land is heavily regulated by federal officials. Second, few tribes other than the Pueblos have obtained rights to land from foreign nations, and the Treaty of Guadalupe Hidalgo pledged U.S. protection to the Pueblos. Finally, the Pueblos have remained highly traditional and are well known for their industriousness and close church affiliation.

In any event, the Pueblos have been spared much of the harm that other tribes have suffered at the hands of the federal government. No Pueblo was ever forced to sign a treaty with the United States. In addition, not a single piece of Pueblo land was removed under the General Allotment Act of 1887, although few other reservations were spared. It is obvious that the Pueblos enjoy a special status with the federal government.

ALASKA NATIVES

What is the historical background of the native inhabitants of Alaska?

The land that is now the state of Alaska has long been inhabited by three groups of people: the American Indians, the

Eskimos, and the Aleuts. When Alaska was purchased from Russia in 1867, its native population was scattered in 200 villages, located principally along the southern and far northwestern coasts. Hunting and fishing were the main sources of livelihood, as they are today, although oil development has benefitted a few villages..

Until recently, Congress dealt with the Alaska Natives in the same manner as with most other Indian groups. The Citizenship Act of 1924, which extended United States citizenship to all Indians born in the United States, expressly included the Eskimos, Aleuts, and Indians of the Alaska Territory. Likewise, Alaska Natives were allowed to participate in the Indian Reorganization Act of 1934 (this was discussed in chapter 6), and more than 70 tribes have organized under the IRA. Most other federal Indian laws apply to the native people of Alaska, and Alaska Natives have been recognized as having a trust relationship with the United States, entitling them to all the programs and services that Congress has made available to Indian tribes generally.

Like the Pueblos of New Mexico, no treaties were ever signed between the United States and any Native group of Alaska. This is largely because, until recently, few whites wanted to live in Alaska, and there was no conflict over land.

In what respects do the Alaska Natives have a unique relationship with the United States?

In 1955 the Supreme Court was asked to decide whether the Alaska Natives had recognized title (defined in chapter 2) to their homelands or whether their interest was possessory only, that is, whether compensation had to be paid to the Natives if the federal government took their land. In *Tee-Hit-Ton v. United States*, the Court held that the Alaska Natives lacked recognized title and that the federal government could take Native land without paying compensation.

In 1971 Congress passed a comprehensive law regarding the land rights of Alaska's 80,000 native inhabitants. Despite the Supreme Court's decision in *Tee-Hit-Ton*, Congress agreed to compensate the Natives for taking their land and also agreed to give them ownership rights to certain parcels of land. This law, the Alaska Native Claims Settlement Act (ANCSA), changed the nature of the government's relationship with the Alaska Natives.

ANCSA gives Alaska Natives $962.5 million in compensation for extinguishing all of their land claims, and in addition, it gives them ownership rights to 40 million acres of land. Of this 40 million acres, 22 million were divided among the 200 Native villages according to their population, with each village selecting the land it wanted to live on. The remaining 18 million acres, as well as all the minerals, oil, and other resources located beneath the entire 40 million acres, were given to twelve Native regional corporations. (Thus, the 22 million acres given to the villages are dually owned: the surface is owned by the village while the subsurface is owned by the regional corporation.) Each Alaska Native is enrolled in a region, based on where he or she lives.

Each person living on December 18, 1971, and possessing one-quarter or more Native blood, was issued 100 shares of corporate stock in his or her regional corporation. ANCSA requires each regional corporation to use its land and resources for the profit of its shareholders. As originally enacted, ANCSA prohibited shareholders from selling their shares for 20 years (until 1991), but thereafter these shares could be sold to any person, including a non-Native. Lands owned by the Native corporation were to be exempt from state and local taxation only during this 20-year period. However, in 1988 Congress amended ANCSA and extended the restrictions on sales of stock and on state taxation indefinitely.

The Native inhabitants of Alaska have a unique relationship with the United States. For one thing, ANCSA gives them extensive rights to land. It places 40 million acres under their direct ownership and control, free from state and local taxation, and provides almost $1 billion in compensation for the land they lost. Congress also has enacted other laws aimed at assisting Alaska Natives. The Alaska National Interest Lands Conservation Act of 1980 (ANILCA) gives the Native population a right to hunt and fish for food. This right takes priority over all other uses of these natural resources. In addition, Alaska Natives and their tribal organizations are entitled to receive the same federal services available to Indians elsewhere in the United States.

The state of Alaska has strongly opposed Native governments and is constantly attempting to limit, or have Congress limit, their powers. Alaska has even taken the position that Native tribes and villages lack the powers of self-government enjoyed by Indian tribes generally. The U.S. Supreme Court has not decided the extent to which Native villages in Alaska may exercise the powers of self-government. However, there is no reason to deny them these powers. Only Congress can strip a tribe of its inherent right of self-government, and Congress has not done so here. This issue, though, is a complex and controversial one, and the Supreme Court eventually will need to resolve it.

OKLAHOMA INDIANS

What is the historical background of the Oklahoma Indians?

The area that is now the state of Oklahoma was given the name Indian Territory around 1830. Originally, Indian Territory was set aside exclusively for Indians. The federal government chose this largely barren land for the relocation of many eastern tribes that were forcibly removed to the West. In essence, it was a dumping ground for Indians whom Congress wanted to move, although at the time, some federal officials truly believed that the Indians would be safer there. Today there are more than 25 tribes located in Oklahoma, few of them indigenous.

The first tribes to be placed in Indian Territory were the Cherokees, Choctaws, Chickasaws, Creeks, and Seminoles. These tribes are often called the Five Civilized Tribes because they had an advanced governmental structure long before the nineteenth century and operated their own schools and courts. Each of the Five Civilized Tribes signed a treaty with the United States in which the tribe was assigned a reservation in Indian Territory. The treaty assured the tribe that its lands would never be taken away, or become part of a state, without the tribe's consent.

The federal government honored this promise until the Civil War. At least two of the Civilized Tribes, the Choctaws and Chickasaws, owned slaves and sided with the Confederacy, and several leaders of the other tribes were sympathetic to the South. After the war, this provided a good excuse for taking tribal lands. Allegedly as a penalty for sympathizing with the Confederacy, all five tribes lost the land they had been assigned in the western portion of Indian Territory. These lands were then assigned to some 20 other tribes, which were all forcibly placed there.

Even after the Civil War, Indian Territory remained officially closed to white settlement, but tens of thousands of whites settled there illegally, and the federal government did little to stop them. By 1907, the non-Indians vastly outnumbered the

Indians, and the territory was admitted into the Union as the state of Oklahoma.

In what ways do the Indians living in Oklahoma have a unique relationship with the United States?

The Oklahoma tribes have a unique relationship with the federal government for just the opposite reason of the Pueblos. Whereas the Pueblos were allowed to retain most of their lands, the tribes in Oklahoma lost most of theirs.

As explained in chapter 1, Congress passed the General Allotment Act in 1887, which authorized the president to sell "surplus" tribal lands to non-Indians. The Five Civilized Tribes were excluded from this law because their treaties with the United States gave them their land outright rather than held it in trust status, owned by the federal government. Nevertheless, Congress wanted these tribes to sell some of their land because non-Indians wanted to live in the area. The tribes refused to do so. In retaliation, Congress passed the Curtis Act in 1898. This act not only forced the Oklahoma tribes to sell most of their land, but it also abolished all tribal courts and removed certain powers of self-government from the tribes, including the right to collect taxes. Some tribes in Oklahoma were left with no land at all.

In 1934, when Congress passed the Indian Reorganization Act, it excluded the Oklahoma tribes from its benefits. Fortunately, in 1936 Congress had a change of heart, and the Oklahoma Indian Welfare Act (OIWA) was passed. The OIWA provides to Oklahoma tribes the same basic benefits as the IRA. For example, it restores their right to establish tribal courts having both civil and criminal jurisdiction.

It is now generally recognized that the Oklahoma tribes possess the same powers of self-government that other tribes enjoy. In addition, the United States has recognized that it has a trust relationship with the tribes of Oklahoma. This entitles them to participate in the federal programs available to other Indian tribes. In 1959, during the termination era (discussed in chapter 1), Congress terminated three Oklahoma tribes—Wyandotte, Peoria, and Ottawa—but restored their federal status in 1977.

Thus, the current situation regarding the Oklahoma tribes is that they have the same general right of self-government, and the same general right to participate in federal Indian programs, as other tribes. However, the Oklahoma tribes were hard hit in past years by Congress, most of their land was taken, and they were placed under extensive federal regulation and control. It has only been in recent years that the federal government, including the federal courts, have begun to protect the interests of the tribes in Oklahoma.

NEW YORK INDIANS

What is the historical background of the New York Indians?

The Europeans who first settled in what is now New York were greeted by the Iroquois Confederacy, the most powerful group of Indians north of Mexico. The confederacy consisted of the Seneca, Cayuga, Onondaga, Oneida, Mohawk, and Tuscarora tribes. The confederacy's territory at one time extended from what we call the Atlantic Ocean to the Mississippi River and from upper Canada into North Carolina, and the confederacy dominated the other tribes in the region.

The Iroquois Confederacy played an important role in the early history of the United States. The confederacy's alliance with Great Britain during the French and Indian War, which ended in 1763, helped assure a British victory over France. During the Revolutionary War, two of the six tribes—the Oneidas and Tuscaroras—sided with the United States, while the others sided with Great Britain. The Oneidas, however, were the most powerful Indian tribe in the Northeast, and their assistance to the colonists was very important.

The treaty that ended the war between the United States and Great Britain was signed in 1783. The next year the United States signed treaties with all six nations of the Iroquois Confederacy. These treaties established boundary lines for the territory of each tribe and recognized each tribe's right to remain free from outside interference.

The United States did not honor these treaties for very long. By the 1820s Iroquois land was highly coveted by non-Indians. The federal government forced many Indians to leave New York and relocate on reservations in Wisconsin and Kansas. The Indians who remained were placed on reservations. Today, there are nine Indian reservations in the state.

In 1790 Congress passed the Indian Nonintercourse Act, which prohibited the sale of Indian land without the federal government's approval. In violation of this law, the state of New York purchased land from various tribes. In recent years, courts have held that these purchases are invalid. This means that these tribes are entitled to money damages for having been deprived of their land illegally. These damages are in the millions of dollars.

In what respects is the relationship between the New York Indians and the federal government unique?

As it turns out, the tribes in New York have a relationship with the federal government similar to that of most other tribes. However, for many years it was believed that these tribes were under the general control of the state government. The confusion began in 1950 when Congress passed a law authorizing New York courts to hear cases involving reservation Indians. This law was interpreted by state officials, and even by many Indians, as authorizing broad state control on Indian reservations in New York.

In 1976, though, the U.S. Supreme Court interpreted an identical law involving other tribes. The Court held that this law did not confer any power on the state in Indian country, except to permit Indians to use state courts if they wanted to. After 1976, then, the presumption was that New York could not exercise civil or criminal jurisdiction over reservation Indians.

This changed again, eight years later. In 1984 Congress passed a law that gives jurisdiction to New York over "all offenses committed by or against Indians on Indian reservations within the State of New York."[1] This law allows New York to arrest and prosecute reservation Indians to the same extent as non-Indians within the state.

Congress has conferred criminal jurisdiction on New York, but not civil jurisdiction, in Indian country. As several court decisions recently confirmed, New York has no greater authority to tax Indians or regulate the use of tribal land than does any other state. (The extent to which a state can exercise civil jurisdiction in Indian country is discussed in chapter 9.) Therefore, while New York Indians are subject to the state's criminal jurisdiction, the tribe controls the activities of Indians on the reservation in virtually every other area of the law.

16

INDIAN GAMING

Most Indian reservations are poor, contain no natural resources of any significance, and offer few opportunities for economic development. The rate of unemployment on most reservations exceeds 70 percent, as compared with about 6 percent in the rest of the country. When combined with such problems as inadequate housing, education, and health care, the living conditions on Indian reservations are the worst in the United States.

In an effort to create jobs and income, some tribes in the 1970s began experimenting with offering high-stakes bingo. Many people love to gamble, and tribal bingo halls were immediately successful, filled mostly with non-Indians. Two tribes located in California, the Cabazon and Morongo Bands of Mission Indians, operated very profitable bingo halls on their reservations, and even added a card club in which draw poker and other card games were offered. The state of California filed a lawsuit against these tribes, claiming that they had to comply with state laws that limited the amount of money that can be waged and the size of prizes that can be awarded in gaming operations.

The case reached the Supreme Court in 1987. In *California v. Cabazon Band of Mission Indians*, the Court held that California had no authority to control Indian gaming on Indian lands because Congress had not given that power to the state. In reaching this decision, the Court noted the importance of providing tribes with this source of income:

> *The Cabazon and Morongo Reservations contain no natural resources which can be exploited. The tribal games at present provide the sole source of revenues for the operation of the tribal governments and the provision of tribal services. They are also the major sources of employment on the reservations. Self-determination and economic development are not within reach if the Tribes cannot raise revenues and provide employment for their members.*[1]

This Supreme Court ruling meant that Indian gaming could not be regulated by any state because no state had been given that power by Congress. This was not good news for the states, which wanted to have some control over this growing industry. As a result, the states pressured Congress to pass in 1988 the Indian Gaming Regulatory Act (IGRA).

The IGRA is complex and detailed, with different rules governing the different types of gaming: bingo, lotto, keno, roulette, slot machines, card games, etc. More than 100 Indian tribes have now complied with these rules and operate gambling halls or casinos in nineteen states. It is estimated that Indian gaming accounts for about 5 percent of the entire gambling industry, generating gross revenues of nearly $6 billion a year.

Some of these tribal casinos are huge. The Foxwoods Casino in Connecticut, owned and operated by the Mashantucket

Pequot tribe on its reservation, is the largest casino in the western hemisphere. Each day, it brings in millions of dollars. The casino is profitable for the tribe as well as for Connecticut. The casino and its related operations (hotel and restaurants) employ nearly 10,000 people, most of whom are non-Indian and therefore pay income taxes to the state. Moreover, the tribe pays taxes to Connecticut on the money waged by non-Indians, and these taxes are estimated to be at least $100 million a year.

Indian gaming is the largest source of economic growth on many Indian reservations and has generated tens of thousands of jobs for Indians and non-Indians. Employment on some reservations is now nearly 100 percent. Not only have tribal members found employment, but they also share in the tribe's gaming profits. The Saginaw Chippewas in Michigan, for example, made $65 million in profits in 1994 from its casino. After paying taxes, it distributed $8,000 per adult and $2,000 per child, and made numerous improvements in its community services. The Mashantucket Pequots have created excellent health-care facilities for tribal members and offer every member a full-tuition education scholarship. Tribes with casinos now have money to build schools, roads, and buildings that will bring their quality of life to a level on par with the rest of the country. The Omaha tribe in Nebraska, for instance, is using some of its casino profits to upgrade the tribe's water system and wastewater treatment facility, and to clean up 22 dump sites on the reservation. These financial successes are all the more astounding given that, until recently, these Indian reservations appeared to have no chance of ever being economically viable. The vast majority of tribes, though, do not have gaming enterprises, and most of them continue to suffer from poverty. Also, many casinos are not very profitable because they are located far from major population centers.

The growing tribal casino industry has had many ramifications, and some tribal members do not appreciate them. Several tribes have voted against having casinos on the reservation, including the largest tribe, the Navajos. Operating a casino on an Indian reservation is likely to cause dramatic changes, including an increase in pollution, traffic, and crime, and will certainly change the quiet way of life familiar to most reservation Indians.

The tribal casino industry has made some enemies. Tribal casinos compete for some of the same tourists who go to Las Vegas, Reno, or Atlantic City to gamble. Some gaming operators in those states have asked Congress to pass legislation limiting these tribal businesses. So far they have not succeeded, but it is difficult to tell what the future will hold.

In 1995 a bill was introduced in Congress which, if passed, would have imposed a 34 percent federal tax on the profits made from tribal gaming enterprises. Tribes lobbied against the bill and pointed out that no similar taxes are assessed against non-Indian gaming businesses. Moreover, for the past century, Congress has said that it wants to improve economic conditions on Indian reservations, and such high taxes would be counterproductive. The bill did not pass in 1995. However, given that Congress is looking for ways to raise money, and given that Indians represent a small portion of the population (and therefore do not have much voting power), such a bill could be enacted in the future. This would be very unfortunate for those tribes that, with gaming, finally have a chance to pull themselves out of the cycle of poverty they have been in since this country placed them on reservations.

Appendix A

The Indian Civil Rights Act
(25 U.S.C. Sections 1301-03)

Section 1301. *Definitions*

For purposes of this subchapter, the term—

(1) "Indian tribe" means any tribe, band, or other group of Indians subject to the jurisdiction of the United States and recognized as possessing powers of self-government;

(2) "powers of self-government" means and includes all governmental powers possessed by an Indian tribe, executive, legislative, and judicial, and all offices, bodies, and tribunals by and through which they are executed, including courts of Indian offenses; and

(3) "Indian court" means any Indian tribal court or court of Indian offense.

Section 1302. *Constitutional rights*

No Indian tribe in exercising powers of self-government shall—

(1) make or enforce any law prohibiting the free exercise of religion, or abridging the freedom of speech, or of the press, or the right of the people peaceably to assemble and to petition for a redress of grievances;

(2) violate the right of the people to be secure in their persons, houses, papers, and effects against unreasonable search and seizures, nor issue warrants, but upon probable cause, supported by oath or affirmation, and particularly describing the place to be searched and the person or thing to be seized;

(3) subject any person for the same offense to be twice put in jeopardy;

(4) compel any person in any criminal case to be a witness against himself;

(5) take any private property for a public use without just compensation;

(6) deny to any person in a criminal proceeding the right to a speedy and public trial, to be informed of the nature and cause of the accusation, to be confronted with the witnesses against him, to have compulsory process for obtaining witnesses in his favor, and at his own expense to have the assistance of counsel for his defense;

(7) require excessive bail, impose excessive fines, inflict cruel and unusual punishments, and in no event impose for conviction of any one offense any penalty or punishment greater than imprisonment for a term of one year or a fine of $5,000, or both;

(8) deny to any person within its jurisdiction the equal protection of its laws or deprive any person of liberty or property without due process of law;

(9) pass any bill of attainder or ex post facto law; or

(10) deny to any person accused of an offense punishable

by imprisonment the right, upon request, to a trial by jury of not less than six persons.

Section 1303. *Habeas corpus*

The privilege of the writ of habeas corpus shall be available to any person, in a court of the United States, to test the legality of his detention by order of an Indian tribe.

APPENDIX B

PUBLIC LAW 83-280
(18 U.S.C. SECTION 1162, 28 U.S.C. SECTION 1360)

Section 1162. *State jurisdiction over offenses committed by or against Indians in the Indian country*

(a) Each of the States or Territories listed in the following table shall have jurisdiction over offenses committed by or against Indians in the areas of Indian country listed opposite the name of the State or Territory to the same extent that such State or Territory has jurisdiction over offenses committed elsewhere within the State or Territory, and the criminal laws of such State or Territory shall have the same force and effect within such Indian country as they have elsewhere within the State or Territory:

State or Territory of	Indian Country Affected
Alaska	All Indian country within the State
California	All Indian country within the State
Minnesota	All Indian country within the State, except the Red Lake Reservation

Nebraska	All Indian country within the State
Oregon	All Indian country within the State, except the Warm Springs Reservation
Wisconsin	All Indian country within the State, except the Menominee Reservation

(b) Nothing in this section shall authorize the alienation, encumbrance, or taxation of any real or personal property, including water rights, belonging to any Indian or any Indian tribe, band, or community that is held in trust by the United States or is subject to a restriction against alienation imposed by the United States; or shall authorize regulation of the use of such property in a manner inconsistent with any Federal treaty, agreement, or statute or with any regulation made pursuant thereto; or shall deprive any Indian or any Indian tribe, band, or community of any right, privilege, or immunity afforded under Federal treaty, agreement, or statute with respect to hunting, trapping, or fishing or the control, licensing, or regulation thereof.

(c) The provisions of sections 1152 and 1153 of this chapter [reproduced in Appendixes C and D of this book] shall not be applicable within the areas of Indian country listed in subsection (a) of this section.

Section 1360. *State civil jurisdiction in actions to which Indians are parties*

(a) Each of the States or Territories listed in the following table shall have jurisdiction over civil causes of action between Indians or to which Indians are parties which arise in the areas of Indian country listed opposite the name of the State or Territory to the same extent that such State or Territory has jurisdiction over other civil causes of action and those civil laws of such State or Territory that are of general application to private persons or private property shall have the same force and effect within such Indian country as they have elsewhere within the State or Territory.

State or Territory of	Indian Country Affected
Alaska	All Indian country within the State
California	All Indian country within the State
Minnesota	All Indian country within the State, except the Red Lake Reservation
Nebraska	All Indian country within the State
Oregon	All Indian country within the State, except the Warm Springs Reservation
Wisconsin	All Indian country within the State, except the Menominee Reservation

(b) Nothing in this section shall authorize the alienation, encumbrance, or taxation of any real or personal property, including water rights, belonging to any Indian or any Indian tribe, band, or community that is held in trust by the United States or is subject to a restriction against alienation imposed by the United States; or shall authorize regulation of the use of such property in a manner inconsistent with any Federal treaty, agreement, or statute or with any regulation made pursuant thereto; or shall confer jurisdiction upon the State to adjudicate, in probate proceedings or otherwise, the ownership or right to possession of such property or any interest therein.

(c) Any tribal ordinance or custom heretofore or hereafter adopted by an Indian tribe, band, or community in the exercise of any authority which it may possess shall, if not inconsistent with any applicable civil law of the State, be given full force and effect in the determination of civil causes of action pursuant to this section.

APPENDIX C

THE GENERAL CRIMES ACT (18 U.S.C. SECTION 1152)

Section 1152. *Laws governing*

Except as otherwise expressly provided by law, the general laws of the United States as to the punishment of offenses committed in any place within the sole and exclusive jurisdiction of the United States, except the District of Columbia, shall extend to the Indian country.

This section shall not extend to offenses committed by one Indian against the person or property of another Indian, nor to any Indian committing any offense in the Indian country who has been punished by the local law of the tribe, or to any case where, by treaty stipulations, the exclusive jurisdiction over such offenses is or may be secured to the Indian tribes respectively.

APPENDIX D

THE MAJOR CRIMES ACT (18 U.S.C. SECTION 1153)

Section 1153. *Offenses committed within Indian country*

(a) Any Indian who commits against the person or property of another Indian or other person any of the following offenses, namely, murder, manslaughter, kidnapping, maiming, a felony under chapter 190A [18 U.S.C. Sections 2241 et seq., i.e., certain sexual offenses including rape and sexual abuse], incest, assault with intent to commit murder, assault with a dangerous weapon, assault resulting in serious bodily injury, arson, burglary, robbery, and a felony under section 661 of this title [18 U.S.C. Section 661, i.e., theft] within the Indian country, shall be subject to the same law and penalties as all other persons committing any of the above offenses, within the exclusive jurisdiction of the United States.

(b) Any offense referred to in subsection (a) of this section that is not defined and punished by Federal law in force within the exclusive jurisdiction of the United States shall be defined and punished in accordance with the laws of the State in which such offense was committed as are in force at the time of such offense.

APPENDIX E

"INDIAN COUNTRY" (18 U.S.C. SECTION 1151)

Section 1151. *Indian country defined*

The term "Indian country," as used in this chapter, means (a) all land within the limits of any Indian reservation under the jurisdiction of the United States government, notwithstanding the issuance of any patent, and, including rights-of-way running through the reservation, (b) all dependent Indian communities within the borders of the United States whether within the original or subsequently acquired territory thereof, and whether within or without the limits of a state, and (c) all Indian allotments, the Indian titles to which have not been extinguished, including rights-of-way running through the same.

NOTES

Decisions of the federal courts are contained in multivolume sets of books known as the Federal Supplement (abbreviated "F.Supp.") for the district courts, the Federal Reporter (abbreviated "F.," "F.2d.," or "F.3d") for the courts of appeals, and United States Reports (abbreviated "U.S.") or Supreme Court Reports (abbreviated "S.Ct.") for the Supreme Court. The names of the parties involved in the case come first, next the volume number, next the name of the reporter, next the page on which the case begins, next the name of the court, and finally the date of the decision. For example, 376 F.Supp. 750 (M.D.Fla. 1974) means that the case appears in volume 376 of the Federal Supplement on page 750 and was decided by the district court for the middle district of Florida in 1974. The librarian at a law school or a library that has law books can help you locate any of the decisions that are cited in this book. The decisions are also available online through Westlaw and Lexis, and through the World Wide Web.

CHAPTER 1

1. A. Josephy, Jr., *500 Nations* (Alfred A. Knopf, New York, 1994), p. 156.

2. R. Strickland, *Genocide-at-Law: An Historic and Contemporary View of the Native American Experience,* 34 *University of Kansas Law Review* 713, 716 (1986).

3. For additional information on the history of federal Indian policy, see F. Prucha, *The Great Father: The United States Government and the American Indians* (Lincoln: University of Nebraska Press, 1984); S. L. Tyler, *A History of Indian Policy,* (Washington, DC: Government Printing Office, 1973), and the extensive bibliography cited at 281–309.

4. The composition and influence of the Iroquois Confederacy is discussed in ch. 15.

5. Act of Aug. 7, 1789, 1 Stat. 50.

6. *Annual Report,* Commissioner of Indian Affairs, 1934, p. 90.

7. H.R. Rep. No. 1804, 73d Cong., 2d Sess., p. 6 (1934). *See also* 25 U.S.C. Sec. 450.

8. 67 Stat. 488, codified as 18 U.S.C. Sec. 1162, 28 U.S.C. Sec. 1360. P.L. 280 is discussed at length in ch. 7.

9. Presidential Documents, Weekly Compilation of, 1968, vol. 4, no. 10 (Washington, DC: Government Printing Office).

10. Message from the president of the United States, 1970, "Recommendations for Indian Policy" (Washington, DC: Government Printing Office).

11. President's Statement on Indian Policy, 1983, Pub. Papers 96, 99 (1984).

12. A. Deer, "Congress Doesn't Say It, but Termination Is the Real Goal," *Indian Country Today,* Sept. 28, 1995, p. A-5.

CHAPTER 3

1. *Cherokee Nation v. Georgia*, 30 U.S. 1 (1831). *See also Worcester v. Georgia*, 31 U.S. 515 (1832); *U.S. v. Kagama*, 118 U.S. 375, 384 (1886); *Seminole Nation v. U.S.*, 316 U.S. 286 (1942).

2. *U.S. v. Mitchell*, 463 U.S. 206, 225 (1983).

3. American Indian Policy Review Commission, *Final Report*, p. 130 (Washington, DC: Government Printing Office, 1977).

4. *Menominee Tribe v. U.S.*, 391 U.S. 404 (1968).

5. This topic has received considerable attention. *See, e.g.*, V. Deloria Jr., *Custer Died for Your Sins* (1969); E. S. Cahn, ed., *Our Brother's Keeper: The Indian in White America* (1969); *Final Report* (note 3 above), pp. 121–38; R. Chambers, *Judicial Enforcement of the Federal Trust Responsibility to Indians*, 27 *Stanford Law Review* 1213 (May 1975).

6. *Final Report* (note 3 above), pp. 106, 127.

7. "Fraud in Indian Country," *Arizona Republic* (Oct. 4, 1987), composite reprint, pp. 1–36.

8. *See Final Report* (note 3 above), pp. 125–36; Chambers, note 5 above.

CHAPTER 4

1. U.S. Const., art. II, sec. 2, cl. 2.

2. U.S. Const., art. VI, sec. 2, provides: "This Constitution, and the laws of the United States which shall be made in Pursuance thereof; and all Treaties made, or which shall be made, under the Authority of the United States, shall be the Supreme Law of the Land; and the Judges in every State shall be bound thereby, any Thing in the Constitution or Laws of any State to the Contrary notwithstanding."

3. *U.S. v. Winans*, 198 U.S. 371 (1905).

4. Cong. Globe, 33d Cong., 1st Sess., App. 202 (1854).

5. *U.S. v. Santa Fe Pacific R.R. Co.*, 314 U.S. 339, 353 (1941).

6. *Federal Power Commission v. Tuscarora Indian Nation*, 362 U.S. 99, 142 (1960) (Black, J., dissenting).

CHAPTER 5

1. For more information on this subject, see: V. Deloria Jr., *Custer Died for Your Sins* (1969); V. Deloria Jr., *Behind the Trail of Broken Treaties* (1974); A. Josephy, *Red Power* (1971); J. Green and S. Work, *Inherent Indian Sovereignty*, 4 *American Indian Law Review* 311; F. Prucha, *The Great Father* (1984).

2. *Worcester v. Georgia*, 31 U.S. 515, 559 (1832).

3. *Johnson v. McIntosh*, 21 U.S. 542 (1823).

4. The Fifth Amendment provides: "No person shall be . . . deprived of life, liberty, or property, without due process of law; nor shall private property be taken for public use, without just compensation."

5. "Fraud," *Arizona Republic*, p. 8.

6. Statement of Ross Swimmer quoted in "Fraud," *Arizona Republic*, pp. 9–11.

7. "Fraud," *Arizona Republic*, p. 3.

8. V. Deloria Jr., *Custer Died for Your Sins*, pp. 60, 81.

9. President Nixon's message to Congress, July 8, 1970, H.R. Doc. No. 91-363, 91st Cong., 2d Sess.

CHAPTER 6

1. *Worcester v. Georgia*, 31 U.S. 515, 557, 560 (1832).

2. 25 U.S.C. Secs. 461 *et seq.*

3. *Santa Clara Pueblo v. Martinez*, 436 U.S. 49, 72 n.36 (1978).

4. *Merrion v. Jicarilla Apache Tribe*, 455 U.S. 103, 137 (1982).

5. *Merrion* (note 4 above), 455 U.S. at 130.

6. *New Mexico v. Mescalero Apache Tribe*, 426 U.S. 324, 333 (1983). *See also Merrion* (note 4 above), 455 U.S. at 144–45.

7. *U.S. v. Wheeler*, 435 U.S. 313, 324 n.15 (1978).

CHAPTER 7

1. U.S. Constitution, art. I, sec. 8, cl. 3. The federal government's authority over Indian affairs is the subject of ch. 5.

2. *McClanahan v. Arizona State Tax Comm.*, 411 U.S. 164, 168 (1973), citing *Rice v. Olson*, 324 U.S. 786, 789 (1945).

3. 25 U.S.C. Secs. 331 *et seq.*

4. 18 U.S.C. Sec. 1162, 28 U.S.C. Sec. 1360.

5. *Washington v. Confederated Yakima Tribes*, 439 U.S. 463, 488 (1979).

6. *California v. Cabazon Band of Mission Indians*, 480 U.S. 202, 216 (1987).

7. *Williams v. Lee*, 358 U.S. 217, 220 (1959).

8. *Ibid.* at 223.

CHAPTER 8

1. *U.S. v. Wheeler*, 435 U.S. 313, 328 (1978). *See also Oliphant v. Suquamish Indian Tribe*, 435 U.S. 191 (1978). This subject is discussed in ch. 6.

2. 18 U.S.C. Sec. 1162, 28 U.S.C. Sec. 1360. P.L. 280 is reproduced in appendix B.

3. 18 U.S.C. Sec. 1152. The General Crimes Act is reproduced in appendix C.

4. 18 U.S.C. Sec. 1153. The Major Crimes Act is reproduced in appendix D.

5. *Denver Post*, Sept. 8, 1985, p. 15A.

6. "Fraud," *Arizona Republic*, pp. 20–22.

7. *Denver Post*, Sept. 8, 1985, p. 14A, citing FBI Director William H. Webster.

8. Unidentified U.S. Department of Justice report, cited in *Arizona Republic* (note 6 above), p. 20.

9. *Washington v. Yakima Indian Nation*, 439 U.S. 463, 470–71 (1979) (citations omitted).

10. U.S. Const., art. IV, sec. 2. The process of extradition is explained in *Pacileo v. Walker*, 449 U.S. 86 (1980).

CHAPTER 9

1. *Williams v. Lee*, 358 U.S. 217 (1959); *Fisher v. District Court*, 424 U.S. 382 (1976); *Merrion v. Jicarilla Apache Tribe*, 455 U.S. 103 (1982).

2. *Washington v. Confederated Tribes of the Colville Indian Reservation*, 447 U.S. 134, 152–53 (1980).

3. *National Farmers Union Ins. Co. v. Crow Tribe of Indians*, 471 U.S. 845, 856 (1985).

4. *McClanahan v. Arizona State Tax Commission*, 411 U.S. 164, 179 (1973).

5. U.S. Const., art. IV, sec. 1.

CHAPTER 10

1. *Squire v. Capoeman*, 351 U.S. 1, 5-6 (1956).

2. *Montana v. Blackfeet Tribe*, 471 U.S. 759, 764 (1985).

3. *Ibid.*

4. *Moe v. Confederated Salish and Kootenai Tribes*, 425 U.S. 463, 483 (1976).

5. *Ibid.*

6. *Merrion v. Jicarilla Apache Tribe*, 455 U.S. 130, 137 (1982).

CHAPTER 11

1. *U.S. v. Winans*, 198 U.S. 371, 381 (1905).

2. *Washington v. Washington State Commercial Passenger Fishing Vessel Ass'n*, 443 U.S. 658, 664–66 (1979) (citations omitted).

3. *New Mexico v. Mescalero Apache Tribe*, 462 U.S. 324 (1983).

4. *Fishing Vessel Ass'n* (note 2 above), 443 U.S. at 666–67.

5. *Ibid.*, 443 U.S. at 696.

6. U.S. Const., art. VI, sec. 2. This clause makes federal treaties and federal laws "the supreme law of the land."

7. *Fishing Vessel Ass'n* (note 2 above), 443 U.S. at 684–85.

CHAPTER 12

1. *Arizona v. California*, 373 U.S. 546, 600 (1963).

2. *Ibid.*

3. *Cappaert v. U.S.*, 426 U.S. 128, 141 (1976).

4. *Washington v. Fishing Vessel Ass'n*, 443 U.S. 658, 686 (1979).

5. *See* note 1 above and the text to which it refers.

6. *Water Policies for the Future—Final Report to the President and to the Congress of the United States*, pp. 474–75 (Washington, DC: Government Printing Office, 1973).

7. H.R. Doc. No. 91–363, 91st Cong., 2d Sess., 10, *reprinted in* 116 Cong. Rec. 23258, 23261 (1970).

Chapter 13

1. In 1924 Congress passed a law, 8 U.S.C. Sec. 1401(a)(2), that extended United States citizenship to all Indians born in the United States, although some Indians became citizens earlier in treaties with the United States.

2. 42 U.S.C. Chap. 21B.

3. S.J. Res. 102, Aug. 11, 1978, Pub. L. No. 95-341, 92 Stat. 469, *codified in part* 42 U.S.C. Sec. 1996.

4. *Liberty and Justice for All*, U.S. Commission on Civil Rights. Report by the South Dakota Advisory Committee (Oct. 1977).

5. C. Wilkinson, "Several Myths Muddy Understanding of Indian Fishing Dispute," *Oregon Journal* (July 20, 1976), p. 10.

6. Public Law 101-601, 104 Stat. 3048 (1990).

Chapter 14

1. 113 Cong. Rec. part 26, p. 35473, 90th Cong., 1st Sess. (Dec. 7, 1967) (statement of Sen. Hruska [R. Neb.]).

2. S. Rep. No. 841, 90th Cong., 1st Sess. 6 (1967).

3. The Fifteenth Amendment states in pertinent part: "The right of citizens of the United States to vote shall not be denied or abridged by the United States or by any State on account of race, color, or previous condition of servitude."

4. 25 U.S.C. Sec. 1302.

5. 25 U.S.C. Sec. 1302(7).

CHAPTER 15

1. 25 U.S.C. Sec. 232. *See People v. Edwards*, 432 N.Y.S.2d 567 (App. Div. 1980).

CHAPTER 16

1. *California v. Cabazon Band of Mission Indians*, 480 U.S. 202, 218–19 (1987).

RESOURCES

For Further Reading

Nonfiction

American Indians: Answers to Today's Questions by Jack Utter. Lake Ann, Mich.: National Woodlands Pub. Co., 1993. A basic book on current Indian issues.

American Indian Myths and Legends edited by R. Erdoes and A. Ortiz. New York: Pantheon, 1984. An informative book on Indian myths and legends.

American Indian Tribal Governments by Sharon O'Brien. Norman, Okla: University of Oklahoma Press, 1989. A close look at numerous Indian tribes, their history, and their governments. Many maps and photographs.

The Book of Elders edited by Sandy Johnson. New York: HarperCollins, 1994. Thirty American Indian men and women discuss their lives, and their struggles to preserve tradition.

Bury My Heart at Wounded Knee by Dee Brown. New York

and Ontario: Fitzhenry and Whiteside, Ltd., 1970. A "must" for anyone interested in what the U.S. government (and the U.S. Cavalry) did to the Indians in the 1800s. An important and well-written book.

Custer Died for Your Sins: An Indian Manifesto by Vine Deloria Jr. Norman, Okla.: University of Oklahoma Press, 1969. A highly critical and insightful look at U.S.-tribal relations.

A History of Indian Policy by S. L. Tyler. Washington, D.C.: U.S. Government Printing Office, 1973. Description (with photographs) of U.S. policies regarding Indians.

Lame Deer: Seeker of Visions by Lame Deer (John Fire) and R. Erdoes. New York: Simon and Schuster, 1972. Personal stories, often humorous, about a Sioux medicine man.

Wisdom's Daughters edited by Steve Wall. New York: HarperCollins, 1993. A special documentation in words and pictures of women Indian spiritual leaders.

Fiction

The Education of Little Tree by Forrest Carter. Albuquerque, N. Mex: University of New Mexico Press, 1976. Award-winning story about an Indian child growing up on a reservation. Despite controversy surrounding the author's personal views regarding Indians, this is a powerful and moving book.

Mean Spirit by Linda Hogan. New York: Atheneum, 1990. Contemporary problems and issues concerning reservation life in Oklahoma written from an Indian perspective.

Reservation Blues by Sherman Alexie. New York: Atlantic Monthly Press, 1995. One of three novels by Mr. Alexie about reservation life, all well-written.

That's What She Said: Contemporary Poetry and Fiction by Native American Women by R. Green (Ed.). Bloomington, Ind.: Indiana University Press, 1984.

Watch for Me on the Mountain by Forrest Carter. New York: Bantam-Doubleday, 1978. A novel tracing the life and military strategies of Apache leader Geronimo.

ORGANIZATIONS

National Congress of American Indians (NCAI)
2010 Massachusetts Avenue NW
2nd Floor
Washington, DC 20036
Tel: (202) 466-7767
Fax: (202) 466-7797

NCAI is the oldest and largest general-purpose Indian organization. It seeks to promote and protect the rights of Indian tribes and individuals.

National Indian Law Library (NILL)
1506 Broadway
Boulder, Colorado 80302
Tel: (303) 447-8760
Fax: (303) 443-7776

NILL contains one of the largest collections of research information on Indian affairs. Though understaffed, they try to answer requests for information.

Native American Rights Fund (NARF)
1506 Broadway
Boulder, Colorado 80302
Tel: (303) 447-8760
Fax: (303) 443-7776

1712 N Street NW
Washington, DC 20036

Tel: (202) 785-4166
Fax: (202) 822-0068

310 K Street
Suite 708
Anchorage, Alaska 99501
Tel: (907) 276-0680
Fax: (907) 276-2466

NARF, headquartered in Boulder, Colorado, is a nonprofit organization specializing in the protection of Indian rights. The priorities of NARF are:

1. Preservation of tribal existence;
2. Protection of tribal natural resources;
3. Promotion of human rights;
4. Accountability of governments to Native Americans; and
5. Development of Indian law.

Americans for Indian Opportunity (AIO)
681 Juniper Hill Road
Bernalillo, New Mexico 87004
Tel: (505) 867-0278
Fax: (505) 867-0441

AIO is a national Indian-advocacy organization that assists tribes and individuals in areas such as natural resources development, justice, and education.

ARROW, Inc.
1000 Connecticut Avenue NW
Suite 1206
Washington, DC 20036
Tel: (202) 296-0685
Fax: (202) 659-4377

Resources

ARROW (Americans for the Restitution and Righting of Old Wrongs) is a nonprofit, tax-exampt, charitable and welfare organization. Founded in 1949, ARROW is dedicated to direct aid, training, and research for American Indians. ARROW also provides program and financial management for the Native American Development Corporation.

Council of Energy Resource Tribes (CERT)
1999 Broadway
Suite 2600
Denver, Colorado 80202
Tel: (303) 297-2378
Fax: (303) 296-5690

CERT is an organization of Indian tribes that own oil, gas, coal, or other energy resources. It enables member tribes to share ideas and experiences and to speak collectively on energy-related matters. It also provides technical assistance to tribes.

HONOR (Honor Our Neighbors' Origins and Rights, Inc.)
2647 North Stowell Avenue
Milwaukee, Wisconsin 53211
Tel: (414) 963-1324
Fax: (414) 963-0137

1425 44th Street NW
Washington, DC 20007
Tel: (202) 333-0474
Fax: (202) 333-0474

HONOR, headquartered in Milwaukee, Wisconsin, is a national ecumenical and secular human-rights coalition that focuses on Native American issues. Members, Indian and non-

211

Indian, stand together as allies seeking justice on critical concerns facing Native Americans today. HONOR was formed in 1988 in response to attacks on Indian lands, people, sovereignty, and treaties. Its information clearinghouse, action alerts, and organizing provide tools for advocacy.

INDEX

Stephen L. Pevar is a national staff attorney for the American Civil Liberties Union, a position he has held since 1976. In addition, Mr. Pevar is an adjunct professor at the University of Denver School of Law, where he teaches a course titled Indian Law. From 1971 through 1974, Mr. Pevar was a Legal Services attorney on the Rosebud Sioux Indian Reservation in South Dakota. He has litigated many Indian rights cases. Mr. Pevar graduated from Princeton University in 1968 and from the University of Virginia School of Law in 1971. Mr. Pevar is married to Laurel Hoskins, and they have two daughters, Lianna and Elena.